T5-AOB-087

Sept 8, 94

To Bob. May the life of Br John G. Hanning. be an inspiration

The Man Who Got Even With God

to follow in his search to find God. and to grow in the love & devotion of Jesus, our Lord

With God's blessing
Father Paschal
abbot

THE MAN WHO GOT EVEN WITH GOD

M. Raymond, O.C.S.O.

St. Paul Books & Media

Cum permissu Reverendissimi Domini,
HERMANNI-JOSEPH SMETS,
Abbatis Generalis Ordinis Cisterciensium
Strictioris Observantiae

Nihil Obstat: M. ALBERT WULF, O.C.S.O.
M. MAURICE MALLOY, O.C.S.O.
Censores

Imprimi potest: + FREDERICK M. DUNNE, O.C.S.O.
Imprimatur: + JOHN A. FLOERSH, D.D.

Cover credit: Tom Dusterberg

Library of Congress Cataloging-in-Publication Data

M. Raymond, Father, O.C.S.O., 1903-
   The man who got even with God / Fr. M. Raymond.
     p. cm.
   ISBN 0-8198-4724-0 (pbk.)
   1. Hanning, John Green. 2. Trappists—United States—
Biography.
I. Title.
BX4705.H245M18 1988
271'.125'024—dc19
[B]
                                      87-33239
                                            CIP

Copyright © 1988 by the Daughters of St. Paul

Printed in the U.S.A., by the Daughters of St. Paul
50 St. Paul's Ave., Boston, MA 02130

St. Paul Books & Media is the publishing house of the Daughters of St. Paul, an international congregation of women religious serving the Church with the communication media.

2 3 4 5 6 7 8 9   95 94 93 92

To
my Mothers
Mary of Nazareth
Queen of Heaven
and
M.B.F.
Queen of my Heart
with
all my
Love and Devotion

Contents

Preface	11
Forewarned	15
Kentucky Temper	23
Southern Fires	31
Down by the Rio Grande	43
His Old Kentucky Home	57
The Last Man in the World	73
The Irresistible and the Immovable Meet	99
A Member of the Lost Battalion	117
Metanoia—The Molding of a Man	131
The Deepening of a Heart	147
Falling in Love	169
Heart Pearls	189
Joachim "Gets Even" with God	205
God "Gets Even"	223
Foreclosing— Joachim Speaks for Himself	235

Preface

IS THE GRACE OF GOD REAL?—YES!
How real?

It changed a tempestuous and turbulent cowboy into a meek and gentle saint.

Where?—When?—How?

Where?—Abbey of Gethsemani. When?—Just a few years ago. How?—Trappist Rule.

Trappist Rule?—I know what a cowboy is, but what is a Trappist? Is he someone who makes traps and hunts game?

Yes—just that—but not the traps you are thinking of, nor the game you are imagining. Listen—I'll tell you what a Trappist is. You are going to be surprised.

Way back in the third and fourth centuries, grand, heroic men, athirst to be alone with God alone and for God alone, left city and town to live in desert solitudes in Egypt and Asia and Palestine. For better protection and supervision, they later gathered into groups under a superior or abbot.

In the fifth century St. Benedict in Italy wrote a rule for such communities. In the course of centuries modifications crept in, which softened the original spirit. In the twelfth century a Benedictine monastery was founded in Citeaux, France, as a successful attempt to live St. Benedict's Rule without those modifications. This was the origin of the monasteries of the Cistercian Order.

As the centuries passed on, again modifications crept in. In the seventeenth century De Rance, Abbot of a Cistercian monastery at La Trappe, France, once more succeeded in restoring in his abbey the Rule of St. Benedict, as originally written. In the nineteenth century, in the month of December, 1848, the first Trappist monastery in the United States of America was founded at Gethsemani, Nelson County, Kentucky.

Thus, Trappist life is not a creation of the twelfth or the seventeenth centuries, but it is the most primitive form of monasticism now in existence in the Western Church. A Trappist monastery is a small section of the Old World of the fifth century transplanted and vigorously flourishing in the New World of the twentieth. There, day by day, at Gethsemani, over a hundred and twenty monks under their Reverend Father Abbot, continue the primitive simplicity and centuries-old traditions of the Rule of

St. Benedict as he originally wrote it, fifteen hundred years ago.

A Trappist is a trapper, and hunts game. But the traps he sets are spiritual ones to catch the devil; the game he hunts are human souls; the Master he works for is Jesus, the "Hound of Heaven," and as for the monk himself, if he works like John Green Hanning—he becomes a saint.

But what does a Trappist do?

He lives the liturgical life of breviary and missal, around the cycle of the year, at daily Mass, Holy Communion, and Divine Office. He earns his bread in the sweat of his brow, in barn, field and forest. He nourishes his mind with readings from Holy Scripture, from the Fathers, and from the lives of the saints. He reinvigorates his soul with mental prayer. He keeps Jesus company in sweet visits to the Blessed Sacrament. He develops kind charity in brotherly love for his fellow monks. And all this he does in an atmosphere of silence, solitude, seclusion, joy, peace, and rest.

A Trappist lives a life hidden far from the eyes of the world, but a life of tremendous supernatural value and importance to the world. Many moderns cry at the Trappist monks: "Why this waste?"

Pius XI replies for the Trappists: "Such hidden victims do not lead useless lives, nor do they belong to an age of bygone Catholicity.... Today above all are such men needed. For those who fulfill the duty of prayer and penance contribute much more to the growth of the Church and the saving of souls than those who labor in the active vineyard."

John Green Hanning became one of these monks. He gave to his God not just the fruit, but the root, trunk, and branches of his life. He gave all and won all—the only All—the eternal All—God. In a grand, heroic, enthusiastic, complete sacrifice of self—as a Trappist monk, he proved that even if cowboys become Trappists, they, too, can become saints—by the grace of God.

Frederick M. Dunne, OCSO,
Abbot of the Abbey of Gethsemani

Forewarned

I am not going to foreword this book. I am going to forewarn you. I want you to meet a "Southern gentleman," a real, American, Southern gentleman. I know that you will say, "Pleased to meet you," because you are polite; but when the interview is over, you will say, "Glad to have met you, very glad!" and from a heart that is full. You may not like him at first, but I do beg you to be patient and to persevere. You cannot judge a book by its cover, nor a man by the boy that he was. One swallow does not make a spring, nor a gray dawn a dreary day. John Green Hanning, the man, is an inspiration, and inspiration we all need. John Green Hanning, the boy...well, that is another story.

Leon Bloy has said, "There is only one sorrow—not to be a saint." We all know that Bloy is right and so we are all sorrowful. Sanctity seems so far from us, so impossible to us. We know what a saint is and what a saint does and also what we are and what we do; hence, we just about despair. That is why we must meet John Green Hanning. He will help us. John was not born a saint—far from it. John was not a saint in his youth—very far from it. But John became a saint, and therefore I must tell you his story.

It seems to me that saints are given us entirely for our encouragement. And my proof? Listen. I do not admire St. Peter denying our Lord and swearing, nor his wavering faith as he walked on the waters. But both his denial and his hesitation help me on to sanctity. I have faltered and fallen; and if I cannot weep as Peter did, I can at least cry out: "Lord, save me, I am perishing." I do not admire Saul holding the coats of those who stoned St. Stephen, nor riding from Jerusalem to Damascus breathing threats against all Christians. Saul was a hateful and hate-filled individual. But Saul become Paul gives me courage. If he could change such hate to love, I have hopes.

And so it is with many others—in fact, with almost all the other saints. Their initial weakness gives me strength and their final sanctity, inspiration. I thank God for Magdalene, the sinful, who became Mary the Christ-loving; for Augustine, the sinner, who became Augustine the saint; and for Alphonsus, who at eighty could say to a woman, "If we are going to talk, let us keep the table between us. I have blood in my veins." I thank God for all those who were human but who by cooperation, by personal endeavor, by real work became divine. I thank God especially for John Green Hanning, the American Trappist, and I feel sure that you will do the same before you have finished this book.

It has been said that "a great person is what we all would be if we could; a great saint is what we all could be if we would." That sounds like a mere play on words, but it is more, very much more than that. It is the deepest of deep truth and easily deducible from revelation. Has not St. Paul said: "This is the will of God—your sanctification"? Are we going to say that God has given us the materials for the building but denied us the plans? Hardly. God never does things by halves, nor ever does half a thing. The materials that he has given us—raw, very raw, materials—are our natures; the plans—people like John Green Hanning.

But here I must warn you as does Father C. C. Martindale, S.J., that we are to imitate the saints, not reproduce them. We are to duplicate their principles, not their acts. To be like Paul we do not need a horse and a ride to Damascus; we need only a heart. We need not be shipwrecked and a "day and a night in the sea"; we need not preach to the gentiles nor write masterly epistles; all we need is to let "nothing separate us from the charity of Christ" and by leading our ordinary Catholic lives "preach Christ and him crucified." To be like Peter we do not have to be crucified head downward; we merely have to have faith as rocklike as Gibraltar. To be like Magdalene we need no alabaster box, beautiful hair, nor Simon's house; we have the confessional, and the tabernacled Christ. To be like John Green Hanning we need not become Trappists, but merely use the nature God has given us, follow the Way of the Cross and the Rosary, and be vindictive enough to "get even" with God.

This American Trappist will help you and me, because most of us are destined and predestined to lead just common, ordinary lives. There are always more soldiers than generals, more people than presidents, more dandelions than orchids. There are always more ordinary, simple souls than scintillating saints, and because most of us are not going to scintillate, we need to meet and to know *The Man Who Got Even With God*.

In *The Ungrateful Beggar*, Leon Bloy says: "We become nothing, not even a blockhead. If a man is not the greatest artist in the world before he has ever drawn a line, he will never become it." In a certain sense, Bloy is right; in another very certain sense, Bloy is exceedingly wrong. Predestination is a fact, but it is also a fact that we "must work out our salvation"; and the accent is on "we" and on "work."

Christ wrought our Redemption, but we must endorse the check. Heaven has been opened for us, but we must walk in, and the only two feet we have to walk on are the two we are now using. That is the real purpose of this book: to show you that with the two feet you now have, no matter what their condition, you can get to God.

When we become very profound and think deep, deep thoughts about predestination, we should always remember that the mystery of grace is not in the cooperation on our part but in the distribution on the part of God. The unsolvable puzzle is why Saul should be called to evangelize the gentiles and not Stephen. According to our way of reckoning, Saul deserved a stoning and Stephen the elevation to the third heaven. Just why God should use another balance than the one we use will be answered when we are all perfectly balanced—some on the right hand, others on the left, and Christ comes in all his glory. But that Saul *had* to answer, "Lord, what will you have me do?" or that Stephen *had* to kneel down and pray for his murderers, is nonsense. Saul could have flamed into fury when he found himself sitting on the Damascus road instead of on his horse, and Stephen could have apostatized when the stones began to fly. But Saul *became* Paul and Stephen *became* St. Stephen because they cooperated with the grace given them. And so for us all; we must *become* as great in our own degree as Paul and Stephen, and the only way is by work.

Leon Bloy should remember that we are born babies and not blockheads, and to *become* a *good* blockhead we must work with the grace that God gives us.

Bloy wants blockheads to become good blockheads, and I want you to know and be like John Green Hanning.

There is another and a subtler purpose for this book, and yet it is so closely related to the former that it can hardly be called "another." It is this. For some unknown reason Europeans think that Americans cannot be decent Catholics, let alone real contemplatives. Such a delusion would be laughable were it not so contagious. But somehow or other this European virus has entered our blood and begotten in us a spiritual "inferiority complex." We think that we Americans can be good money-makers, but never good mystics; good workers, but never good worshipers; very active Catholics, but never true contemplatives; that since we are Americans, we are destined to be producers and not pray-ers, energetic builders of skyscrapers, but never silent souls building the Mystical Body of Christ up to the very heavens. We seem to think that by our birth in this land of materialism and excessive activity we are doomed to spiritual mediocrity. We are determined not to be great sinners, but we are not determined to be great saints...because we are afraid! It is a poison that has gotten into our very souls. John Green Hanning will help to get it out.

If ever a man was an American, he is the man. He was born and bred in old Kentucky. As a boy he witnessed the Civil War, saw Lincoln free the slaves and unite a nation; as a young man he went to Texas and became a real American cowboy at a time when only real Americans became real cowboys; in his later years he returned to his native state, and died at Gethsemani's Abbey, not far from his old Kentucky home. Yes, John Green Hanning was all-American, and he became—well, read the story.

Just one last word of warning and then we will plunge into our story. I am going to show you a vindictive soul, but do not be too easily shocked—vindictiveness is close to virtue, very close, just as hate is close to love. I know well that they are opposites, and yet the closest thing to love is hate, and the closest to sterling justice and heroic retribution is vindictiveness.

When the lily first puts its head above the ground, you cannot tell it from an onion. When a boy in his early years shows stubbornness, you cannot tell whether he will become a man of strong determination or a bully. So, too, with "getting even": it can make a man a murderer or a glory to Jesus Christ! We all have that little mean streak in us. We all like to "get even," and that is precisely why this life of John Green Hanning must be written—to show us what we can do with that urge.

Kentucky Temper

"I'll get even. I always do." It was John Green Hanning talking and, though he did not know it, he was summing up his whole character and his whole manner of life. The blazing blue eyes that flashed anger and the boyish jaw that set so firm told their own story of southern fire. John was a Kentuckian, and Kentuckians have always been noted for their temper.

The bell for class had rung and brown-robed Trappist lay brothers were ushering in the orderly files to "The Monks' School" which stood so commandingly on the top of a Gethsemani hill. If that bell had not rung or if brown-robed lay brothers were not present, John Green Hanning, now looking like a volcano, would be erupting. He had been tripped. It was only the ordinary schoolboy trick, but John would not see the joke. He could not stand being laughed at, and the smiles on the faces of his classmates deepened the scowl on his own, as he kept muttering, "I'll get even. I always do."

Whether he "got even" or not does not really interest us, but what does catch our fancy and causes us to wonder is the flash we get of this boy's character. It is the year 1865 and John Green Hanning is just sixteen—a fascinating age, a frightening age. The boy has fire. Will the man be a conflagration or a furnace? Will he devastate or radiate? These questions leap to mind. Time and John Green Hanning alone will answer.

Born on January 12, 1849, he saw the light of day in Lebanon, Kentucky, just three weeks and a day from the founding of the first Trappist Abbey in America at Gethsemani, not so many miles away. But the monks knew nothing of John's arrival and, of course, John paid no attention to the monks. He was born in a cold month, but from January 12, 1849, to the end of time—and even after it—this son of John Hanning and Mary Jane Hagan was to be a blaze.

John Hanning and Mary Jane Hagan were happy that day, because for the fourth time God had blessed their union with a child. John Senior was proud that January day but not so proud as John Junior; the elder strutted like a peacock and the younger announced in no subdued tones that he had arrived. And Mary Jane, looking from John in her arms to John at her side, wondered which was the bigger baby.

After the intoxication of the moment, John and Mary Jane thanked God for his blessing, and as soon as possible had the parish priest make their little son God's child with the waters of Baptism. Thus, John Green Hanning was born again and from a mere Kentuckian became a Kentucky Catholic and from just an American, he became an all-American child of God.

This new son of God and John Hanning would cause both his heavenly father and his earthly many a worry and many a pain before he became a real man, for there slumbered within this baby boy Vesuvian fires. With his mother it would be different. He would love her and love her always. His love for his mother was, next to his faith, God's greatest gift to him. It held him from the deepest depths and guided him home. Although I cannot say just when John Green Hanning's love for his mother was born, I can say it never died. John was going to see many strange places and many strange faces before he finally settled down. He was going to wander far from home and family, but one pair of eyes that would never fade from memory were the eyes that saved his soul—the eyes of his mother.

But I am ahead of myself. Before we land

in Europe we must leave New York, and here I am almost at the end of my story before I have left the beginning. There is no sense in giving the answer before we have put the question, is there? It is like giving the solution before proposing the problem.

Let us go back to our sixteen-year-old Southerner just filing into Gethsemani College. Yes, I am starting with John at sixteen instead of six and for two very good reasons. First, I know nothing of him at six; second, I do not care for "baby saints." In fact, I do not believe in "baby saints"! Of course, if that is heresy, I will retract it, but if it is what I think it is, namely, sound common sense based on sounder theology, I will insist upon it. No, I do not believe in "baby saints" except, perhaps, John the Baptist, if, as we may suppose, he had the use of reason when he leaped in his mother's womb, and, of course, Mary Immaculate. The evangelists were excellent hagiographers and wrote real lives of real saints. They show us men and women who became saints, not men and women who were born saints. They show us the hardheaded Simon who became the daring Peter, the hating Saul who became the zealous Paul, the passionate and sensuous Magdalene who became the spiritual and silent Mary, and so on for a whole host of other men and women. And all are men and women of flesh and blood, of faults and failings, of anger and temper, just like you and me. They give me courage. How about you?

As I have said, the sacred writers give us nothing of the baby days and the baby ways of these people, and there is an obvious reason. After all, to be saintly, one has to conform to the will of God; and for this one must know the will of God. Can a baby who has the ownership but not the use of senses and intellect know the will of God? What is the use of talking? The infallible Church says that ordinarily the use of reason is attained at seven years; and let me add that there is a vast difference between coming to the *age* of the use of reason and coming to the use of reason. Just as much of a difference as there is between being twenty-one and being an adult. All humans, if they live long enough, will reach the age of maturity, but not all humans, no matter how long they live, will mature.

All of which brings me back again to John Green Hanning at sixteen and not at six. John was a boy, a real boy; in fact, he was all boy. Physically he was average sized, tending more to the thin and wiry type than to the husky or the tall. Intellectually he was neither a genius nor a dullard—just the ordinary, quick-witted, fully-alive American boy. Spiritually? Well, all the marks given him at the monks' school for his two semesters were "very good." He was "very good" in punctuality, in deportment, in piety, in application. In fact, judging from the school record, we would have to say that John was a "very good" boy. But the monks did not mark for temper, nor for quarrelsomeness, nor for the spirit of "getting even"! If they had, then in place of "very good" they would have written "excellent." John had an excellent temper, if we judge a temper's excellency by the frequency of its outbursts and the violence of its eruptions. John was an excellent quarreler, if an excellent quarreler is one who always walks around with a "chip on his shoulder" ready to fight if it falls off, let alone if it is knocked off. And above all, John was most excellent in "getting even"! He admitted it himself. He said that he "always got even."

But perhaps I am misleading. John Green Hanning was not Peck's original "bad boy," nor the real "bad boy" of his school. In fact, John Green Hanning was not a bad boy but an American youngster, raised in old Kentucky at the time of the Civil War. That is important, very important. For war days affect a nation down to its last war baby, and post-war days are worse. War days are abnormal days. Hysteria grips a nation, so that unbiased judgment and sound, balanced thinking become impossible. Truth is boycotted and banished, while lies, masquerading under the name of propaganda, are broadcast the length and breadth of the land. Instead of giving "all the news that's fit to print," the newspapers give us only the news that is print to fit—to fit the policy of the ruling party, to fit the pulse of the people. Emotion replaces thought; passion and prejudice parade as virtues.

All this is doubly true of the Civil War. From 1860 to 1864 our country was in an abnormal condition and livid with seething passions. Of all states Kentucky was the most abnormal. Situated on the borderline between the North and the South, she had her slave sympathizers and her slave owners, soldiers in blue and soldiers in gray, heroes under Lee and heroes under Grant. The result was inevitable: neighbors ceased to be neighbors; brothers to be brothers; fathers were fighting against their sons, and sons against their fathers.

In such an atmosphere John Green Hanning grew up. Whatever previous combativeness and determination never "to be bested" he may have had were now accentuated. War days produce paradoxical effects. They submerge the individual and yet bas-relief his invividuality. They dragoon people into a heroic forgetfulness of self and yet make them startlingly self-conscious. They effectively merge men into a fighting unit and yet make them all the more conscious of their individuality and independence. There follows, as a consequence, the surge of individualism and independence so conspicuous in postwar days. Thus it was that John Green Hanning's independence and self-assertivenes grew. The Civil War effected his Kentucky temper.

Southern Fires

We are going to leave John Hanning's school days, but before we do, let us note that John was not first in his class, nor a teacher's pride and joy. He was not outstanding for piety or prudence; nor was he the leader or model of his group in any sense of the word. That is one too many negatives and so here is a positive. John Green Hanning was just like you and me: ordinary. He was an average American boy of sixteen, who came up to standard in all things but distinguished himself in nothing.

If John Green Hanning is ever canonized, he should be called "the ordinary saint" and hailed immediately as the patron of the average man. But even now he should appeal to you, to me, and to all ordinary people, because he is one of us. What makes him especially appealing is his extraordinary lack of the extraordinary. As a boy John had neither halo, visions, ecstasies, nor outstanding virtues. He was just an American Catholic boy, normal in all save his temper, and even that for Kentucky was almost normal.

But before we leave John Hanning's school days, I must tell you that when John was sixteen and had completed only one semester at Gethsemani College, he said to his father, "Dad, may I become a Trappist monk?"

"A what?" roared his father.

"A monk!" shouted the reddening John Green.

"Listen, lad," said the father, "they don't take in babies at the monastery."

It was John Green's turn to roar, but instead he only sulked and pouted, "Who's a baby?"

"You are," said his father. "You're just sixteen, and you're talking about becoming a Trappist, a life only for men. That's baby talk."

Young John flushed and fumed, but he did not leave his father's side. If anyone else had said it, there would have been a fight. But John Green, respecting his father, just blushed and kept silent.

The silence grew painful to both parties, so the father finally said, "If you are waiting for a more definite reply, here it is. You may not become a Trappist now, and perhaps never. So run along and forget your mad dream.

You're too young to be thinking about such things anyhow."

John ran along and forgot about it, but only because John had something else to think about. He was wondering what makes a boy a man, and why sixteen isn't old enough to be mature. John Green Hanning was mad—mad with his father for calling him a baby and with himself for being "just sixteen."

We take up our story four years later. John is not quite a man according to law, but too much of a man according to his own mind. We find him on a tobacco farm in Lebanon, Kentucky—for to Lebanon his folks had moved for very substantial reasons. "Stick to your cloth" is good advice for most tailors, but not for all tailors, in the opinion of Mrs. Hanning. The needle and the shears had brought her husband a tidy fortune, but also too many unfortunate "friends." These, finding that John Hanning, Sr., not only had an open heart but also an open hand, took advantage of both. Irishmen are cut out for many things, but never for moneylenders; so Mrs. Hanning persuaded her genial and generous husband to leave Lebanon and tailoring and become a tobacco raiser. In 1857, 1000 acres of good land were purchased and the Lebanon tailor became the Owensboro tobacconist.

This chapter will not tell you much about

life on a tobacco farm, because if you have lived on or near one, you know more about it than I do; if you have never seen one, then the little given will not help greatly. However, there is one thing that I must tell you, for without it this chapter would be as sensible as Hamlet without a problem or the Merchant of Venice without his pound of flesh. Tobacco, long before it becomes a cigar or a cigarette, a "Corona-Corona" or a "Camel," is hung up in barns. Now that is important; important for the tobacco, important for the cigar or the cigarette, and most important for this chapter. The barn is not for storing purposes but for the mellowing processes. In it the tobacco leaf is hung up to dry and to gain that delightful aroma which makes a five-cent cigar cost fifteen cents. Hence you can readily see that the barn is to the tobacco farm, what the mint is to the United States Treasury. With that clearly grasped, proceed with the story.

One day John Hanning, Jr., and John Hanning, Sr., had a misunderstanding which grew into a bitter clash as two strong characters met in fierce opposition. John Senior was determined; John Junior, more so. The father was convinced that this was the psychological moment to break the stubborn will of his son, who, though only one year from full manhood, showed as much maturity as a young colt and much more obstinacy. The son was equally convinced that this was just the moment to show his father that he had a will of his own and that he was no longer a mere boy. The father grew silent; the son grew sullen.

The sun went down that day on their silence and their sullenness. Somehow John Junior felt that he had been wronged, humiliated, outraged. With each hour of moroseness and self-pity, his anger mounted. At sunset he was seeing red, as flame blazed in his heart and fire seethed through his brain. As the stars came out, John Green Hanning had ceased to think. His heart and brain beat with that numbing, ceaseless, maddening chant, "I'll get even! I'll get even! I'll get even!"

The lights went out in the Hanning home that night and peace held the land, but two hearts were far from peace and two heads were far from rest. The father lay silent and sleepless, staring into the dark, wondering how best to break the will of his boy and make him a man. The son lay silent and sleepless, peering into the dark, waiting for the dead of night to show his father that he would not be beaten, that he was a man, that he could "get even."

The hours passed on—slow and seemingly endless hours to the two silent watchers in the dark: sad and perplexing hours for the father, restless and impatient hours for the son. At long last the weary and saddened father closed his eyes. He slept, but not for long, and when he opened his eyes, it was still dark, dark as when he had lain there staring. But looking toward the window, he noticed a brilliant glow in the distance. Half distractedly, he mused... could that be the moon? Hung so low and so golden? But no! It moved, it leaped, it took shape. It was a flame, it was fire! In one leap he was out of the bed and at the window. "The barn! The tobacco barn! Help! Everybody! Fire! The tobacco barn is on fire!"

The entire household—family and hired hands—raced to the blazing building. Buckets, pots, pans, barrels—everything and anything that could hold water—was rushed to the flaming structure. Men and women, boys and girls, worked in frenzy, but all worked in vain. The fire had too great a start and the awkward apparatus for extinguishing it was useless. The barn burned to the ground; the harvest of a year vanished in smoke.

At early breakfast in the Hanning home that morning the sorrowful eyes of a father looked on an empty chair. John Green Hanning was missing. John Hanning, Sr., said nothing. Mechanically he finished breakfast and began the work of the day. All that day, and for many another day, he moved about the farm mechanically. Day followed day, and night, night; and yet the father of the household walked about in silence. The Hanning home was a silent home these days, silent with a silence, not tense like that produced when a patient but powerful man is about to break out in a justifiable rage, but a silence that was sad, caused by the silence of a patient but powerful man whose heart was broken.

The routine work of the farm went on, but only because it was routine work. Were one to watch the owner of the farm at his tasks those days, one would have seen that his hands and his feet were moving but that his mind was very still and many miles away. He was with his boy. Again and again he went over the misunderstanding that they had had and blamed himself for having been too harsh. He cared not about the barn; that could be rebuilt. He cared not about the harvest; next year would give another crop. He cared about his boy. Where was he? What would bring him back?

John Hanning, Sr., was a real father, and during these days, though subconsciously he knew that he had acted the proper part, his heart talked to his head and the tale it told was one of accusation and of forgiveness. He was condemning himself for his harshness and was condoning the sin of his son. Time would lighten the weight on his mind, but nine full years would not take the steel out of his heart.

As for mother, time only deepened the hollow in her soul. Looking at John who was present and looking for John who was absent, trying to be loyal to her husband and not untrue to her son, laboring to lighten the leaden heart beside her and praying for the soul of the wanderer, the mother wondered who was the greater sufferer, the sinned against or the sinning. At mealtime her husband often found her staring at an empty chair and when their eyes met, she would grow silent, sigh, and look away. Daily she besought Mary Immaculate to mother her wandering boy. The agony of agonies was not that her son should be so vindictive; she could excuse the sin and love the sinner. The agony of agonies was the silence that deepened with each succeeding day. Yet one thing she knew, that he loved her, and her heart told her that he would return. She was right.

This truth kept her from dying of heartbreak and sorrow during those first months. Yet many were the lonely days and lonesome nights lived by the brave little mother. The loneliest of all lonely days was Christmas. For weeks Mr. Hanning had planned how to make his wife happy. His whole Advent had been a preparation for this day of days, when he was going to show a smiling face and be alive with energy and good cheer.

The day came. Out into the early morning darkness the family went and made its way to church. There in the dim light of the candles and in the sweetness of the tiny crib, quiet and peace were found. During the moving mystery of the Mass, John Hanning, Sr., prayed for strength and wisdom enough to carry off the day; the family prayed for comfort for their mother and Mary Jane Hanning prayed for her boy. Kneeling beside one another, they received Communion and prayed to the little Babe of Bethlehem. Then, as they filed back to their places, the mother hid her head in her hands and talked to Jesus within her heart. What she said only God and herself knew, but one may easily guess that she said much about her boy.

It was a long day for everyone. Bright words flew from mouth to mouth, but they were a bit too bright. The frequent peals of laughter that rang from room to room were a little too loud and a trifle too high to be real. The eager enthusiasm with which everything was done, the presents unwrapped and admired, the table set for dinner, the afterdinner tidying up—all were a little too eager and too enthusiastic. The pleasantries exchanged as evening wore on were tinseled; they glistened, but they were not gold.

At last it was over. The family had retired and mother and father sat alone. "Well, Mary, it's been a happy day, but it's been a long one. Don't you think you should hurry off to bed?"

Then, for the first time that long Christmas Day, was heard Mary Jane Hanning's real voice. She went over and kissed her husband on the forehead, and said, "John, you're a dear. But you don't have to pretend with me."

The last light in the Hanning home went out late that Christmas night, but even in the lonesome darkness a brokenhearted mother was thinking of her boy.

What had happened to her son? On that night of the fire, he had run from the burning tobacco barn with a wild gleam in his eyes. It was a frenzied light, for he was gloating over his deed. Revenge is sweet, very sweet for a while, and as John ran from the blaze he had kindled, he was having that very sweet while. Out toward the southern hills he ran. On a knoll he turned and looked back. The flames were leaping high now and John laughed as he shook his fist in the air. "I'll show him. Now I am even." Then he turned and ran on. On and on into the blackness he ran, with only an occasional look at the glowing sky in back of him. At long last, weary from his exhausting run and worn out from his fiery emotions, he threw himself under a tree and was soon sleeping the sleep of the completely spent.

When he awoke the next morning, he was different. No longer was he the son of a fairly well-to-do tobacco raiser, no longer was he the scion of a highly respected family, no longer was he John Green Hanning just growing into manhood. He awoke to find himself alone and very lonely, to find himself a wanderer, a runaway, a disgrace. He sobered with this realization. The southern fires of his temper were dead.

Down by the Rio Grande

The morning after he had "gotten even," John Green Hanning did some thinking. Quick, superficial, incorrect thinking, but, nevertheless, it was thinking. He thought of what he had done and why he had done it. At first he was inclined to justify himself. In fact, he made every effort to arouse himself to the point of self-approval, but the fires of his temper were dead, and, do what he would, he could not re-light them. He thought of his father and experienced a momentary flash of resentment, but no more than that. He was true to himself, honest, and because of his innate honesty, he slowly admitted that he had wronged a "grand old dad." He thought of his mother, and the tumult of thoughts that tumbled through his mind made him so sick at heart that he refused to think further of home; he resolved to go West.

It was a normal reaction and resolution. Shame, fear, disgrace, and a stupid pride that was a strange combination of cowardice and heroic justice, forced him to this decision. He was afraid to face his father and ashamed to face his mother. He felt that he had so grievously sinned that forgiveness was out of the question. The West was uninviting, but he felt that he had to face it for he had forfeited his right to home. With a shrug of his shoulders that was half resignation and half desperation, he arose and set out for the West.

During the next few months young John Hanning matured more rapidly than he had in all his twenty years past. He was earning his way; he was working for his existence; he was rubbing shoulders, elbows, and hips with life, and he found life both rough and rugged. He posed as a man and was treated as such by men who had neither time nor inclination to be gentle.

After having slept under hedges, in haystacks, and in barns; after having earned a meal from this farmer and from that restaurant keeper; after having learned the art of begging at back doors and arousing the sympathy of cooks; after having stolen rides on hay wagons, with mule teams, and in boxcars, and most especially after having walked and walked and walked, John Green Hanning finally arrived in Texas and there, in the Lone Star State, he became what he had often read about and more often dreamed about...he became an American cowboy.

Often had he thrilled, as he read of brave men who ranged over the prairies on horses that were beauty and grace in action. Often had his young blood risen as he read of keen-eyed, cool, courageous men who swaggered into town with guns swinging from either hip. Often had he exulted, as he read of the heroes of the West who were the incarnation of youth's dream of daring manhood. Now he was one of them, and if ever an individual learned that "truth is stranger than fiction," it was John Green Hanning. He had his horse, he had his guns, he had his swagger, but he also had his work.

Novelists of the "wild West" had never spoken of the endless hours spent in the saddle when the herds had to be moved. They had never told of the merciless, blistering sun, nor of the long and lonely nights, nor yet of the thanklessness of it all. They had made no mention of a hundred and one other things that were part of the life. John often wondered where they had gotten their glamorous notions of the life of a western cowboy.

But it is time to stop calling him John Green Hanning, for he never called himself that, nor was he ever called that. He was known as "the Kentuckian." He had come to a land where few questions were asked and few answered. Applicants were never asked whence they came, nor why they came, nor how long they were going to stay. If they could ride a horse, rope a steer and shoot a rustler, they were hired. Names were more often given in this land than asked for, so our hero became known as "Kentucky Jack," "the Quick One," or simply "the Kentuckian." He had never told anyone he was from Kentucky, but as soon as he had opened his mouth, he had been labeled. The Kentucky twang is just the Kentucky twang, and no one ever mistakes it. The second nickname came because he was still John Green Hanning, the boy with a temper that would flame at the blink of an eye.

Texas from 1869 to 1878 was "the West" and the fairly "wild West." But "the Kentuckian" soon became accustomed to it, and before many months had passed he was a cowboy in every sense of the word. The genuine American cowboy with all his defects was a lovable figure. Primitive in many respects and at times brutal, he also had those redeeming qualities that made the primitive man a man. He had loyalty and cleanness and a rigorous sense of justice. He was upright and honest and, if a "little quick on the trigger," always "above board." He saw very little of the classroom, but he studied in that wider classroom of the range with nature to teach him. The principles that made up his character and guided his life were few yet they were pure.

But do not allow me to canonize the cowboy. He was genuine, but he was crude ore. He was the incarnation of masculinity, and perhaps, because we are such a materialistic and virile people, the lean, leather-skinned rider of the range has become for us somewhat of an idol. Physically he was all that agile America wants. He was as hard as iron and as pliable as a willow. His strength was not the strength of the towering oak; it was rather the unyielding strength of the bendable but unbreakable sapling. Psychologically he was swaggeringly independent, a lover of liberty, and a respecter of the elemental laws. But what makes him most dear is the heart of the American cowboy. At heart he was just a simple child and like all simple children, he was a lover of the simple and sublime.

Someone has well said: "Let me write the songs of a nation and I care not who writes her laws." Let one listen to the songs of a nation, the songs that she really loves, and he is listening to the heart of that nation. So it is with our American cowboy: his soul is in his songs. At heart he was a lover, a lover of the simple and the sublime. Listen to his songs, and you will always hear him singing of love. He sings of his horse, of his saddle and boots, and the dogies he has to drive. He sings of his pals, and of the girl of his dreams. He must sing, for he is often alone and almost always in love.

There is much about nature in cowboy songs, for nature has won the cowboy's heart. Is it any wonder? She is always about him. She caresses him with breeze, on the brow of the hill, just as the day is done. Then she puts on her evening gown and sets stars in her blue-black hair just to bewitch him. All night long she acts the queen and commands tribute to her majesty. But at dawn, the jewels go back in their box, and down tumble her gorgeous tresses. Then abandoning her queenly ways and her queenly walk, nature becomes actually coy. She shows the cowboy the rose of her lips and the dew that has dropped at her toe tops; she scampers and skips through rising mists freshly scenting the world with her fragrance. Small wonder the cowboy falls in love; for nature uses the wealth of her wondrous trousseau and from dawn till dark woos him. Small wonder he lifts his voice in song and incessantly sings of his loved ones.

Coy maiden and queen, nature works a paradox in the riders of the range, as she makes them both hard and soft. She hardens their hands and their bodies, but she softens their boyish hearts. She fills them with sympathy—

not sentiment or still less, sentimentality. Cowboys feel and find a kinship in all things living, and they show it by their manly gentleness to all things. That is the heart—the boyish, loving heart that you will find in the lilting songs of the cowboy.

With such men, then, did John Green Hanning associate for nine full years and by association became one of them. He became a man in body, but remained a boy at heart. And do you ask what happened to his temper? That remained the same; just as violent, just as instantly fired, just as deadly and dangerous. And with it remained that determination always to "get even."

These characteristics remained, but there was one big change in "the Quick One," and that was in the deepening of his heart. When thoroughly analyzed, John Green Hanning had been selfish. His love for his mother was great, but not nearly so great as his love for himself. Now began a deepening process and that heart, that had been so full of self, developed a capacity to love others. It was a slow process, a sly process, but a sure one. The thing that deepened John's heart was silence and song.

Many a night "the Kentuckian" rode the range with only the silent stars and the silent moon for company. Silence provokes thought. It made him enter into himself. But no sooner did he begin to think of John Green Hanning, the cowboy, than he thought of John Green Hanning, the Kentuckian, of his folks at home and all his home surroundings. Then his boyish heart grew hungry. Our wiry, stronghanded rider of the range was becoming homesick, very homesick, and he did not know it.

But silence was not alone in this work of heart deepening. Song did her share. John Green Hanning was blessed with a beautiful natural voice. It was soft, warm, winning and soulful. A voice that commanded silence and attention—one of those voices that everybody loves to hear. There was nothing operatic or dramatic about it, but it was just full of music and melody. It was pure, rich, velvety and vibrant with true feeling. And John Green Hanning loved to use it.

As he rode the range "the Kentuckian" was almost always singing. He had his long cowboy songs and he sang them to their end, but as the years went on he more and more often crooned some Negro folk song or some song genuinely of the South. More and more the distant riders on the range would hear one of those stirring, soul-filled plaintive melodies that very few besides the blacks can either compose or sing. Unknown to himself, the combination of nature's silence and his own singing was deepening his heart and whetting

DOWN BY THE RIO GRANDE 51

his hunger for home. The more he sang to cheer himself, the more did he bring on gloom, for he was always singing songs of the southland. It took nine long years to accomplish its end, but silence and song finally had him once again determined to show them that he always "got even."

Countless were the times during the nine years that he had muttered to himself, "I'll get even. I always do." Bucking broncos learned that the wiry Kentuckian always did "get even." Cattle inclined to stampede or be stubborn found the "Quick One" quick and vindictive. Occasionally his fellows learned that he was not to be trifled with, that he was mighty quick to anger and, if crossed, would always "get even." Yet, the sweetness of revenge was always bitter, for it reminded him of the night that he had flamed a Kentucky sky to "get even," and that memory hurt.

Now comes a deception. John Green Hanning, the Texas cowboy, deceives himself. Nine long years of living close to nature, or riding the wide, wide range by day and by night, had done many things to him. The silence of the day and the deeper silence of the night had talked to him. The loneliness and the emptiness of the prairie and the plain had become filled with visions and with people—always the same visions and the same people, his family and his old Kentucky home. The songs that he sang to lift up his heart only depressed it the more. Finally, while trying to tell himself the truth, John told himself a lie. In what he thought was a fit of anger, he said to himself, "I'll show them! I'll show them! I'll get even. I always do. I'll go home!"

The long silence of his family, who did not know where he was, John seized as a pretext for anger. Foolishly considering himself slighted, he determined to "get even" by going home. It was a grand deception, one that healed many hearts and sanctified many a soul. The truth of the matter is that the boy was showing in the man. John Green Hanning was homesick; he was yearning to see the love of his life, his mother.

So one bright day "the Quick One" gave his rope to a buddy, went out to the corral, put his arm about the neck of his horse and said, "Good-by, old pal," sold his guns and saddle, bought a suit of city clothes, and started for his "old Kentucky home far away." God was being kind to an ingrate.

Have I been too brief in describing these nine years for you? I have not given you the full picture of cowboy life, nor of the life of this particular cowboy. But your imagination can fill in the details. He kept his southern fire and maintained his habit of always "getting even," and from what you know of men, and especially of such men as our early American cowboys, you can give a fairly accurate guess at how many tiffs John Green Hanning had with the men down by the Rio Grande. John did not always win. Nobody always wins. Life is not like that.

But why did I select silence and song to give you the heart of the cowboy? Because this combination was the external grace that God gave to our hero to help him out of the depths. External grace is almost always in the commonplace. It can be anything from a butterfly to Betelgeuse; from the sun, the moon and the sea to a sub-electron. Bugs brought one of our great American scientists to the feet of God and a bursting shell at Pampeluna brought Ignatius Loyola there. Chesterton tells us that he learned from heterodoxy how to be orthodox; he says that he found "in an anarchist club or a Babylonian temple what he might have found in the nearest parish church." But the point is that he found them in these unlikely places; he openly confesses that "the flowers of the field, the phrases heard in an omnibus, the accidents of politics, and the pains of youth, came together in a certain order to produce a certain conviction of Christian orthodoxy." So do not be surprised that I stress silence and song as the elements, the external graces, that remotely helped in the formation of a contemplative from that rawest of raw material...a vindictive cowboy.

Yes, and more than merely vindictive—a God-oblivious ingrate. Some pages back I said that God was being kind to an ingrate. I had much in mind when I wrote that sentence, very much—much that must be told. It is this: John Green Hanning had given up more than his name, his home, and his boyhood habits while he lived down by the Rio Grande. He had given up his God.

Away from church, away from Mass, away from the sacraments, does not necessarily mean away from God. For some it has meant getting closer to God. Among soldiers who seldom saw a chapel or a chaplain, I have met saintly souls, and I know that there have been men of God on the seas. But they are the rare exception. The general run of people need the externals of worship, and very especially do they need the grace of the sacraments and the Sacrifice. And yet, not all who are denied these do what our cowboy did; not all throw away their faith; not all give up their God.

Do you now see how God was being kind to an ingrate, when by silence and song he brought John Green Hanning up from the Rio Grande and into his old Kentucky home? Yes, it was God who did it. About that there is no doubt. The process was slow and imperceptible, but it was most effective. "The Kentuckian" never knew just what it was that turned him to home. He said that he wanted to "get even," but he also admitted that, as the miles between the Rio Grande and his old Kentucky home were being covered, he felt that he was not "getting even" at all; he actually felt that he was getting "odd."

His Old Kentucky Home

As the train clicked and clicked its way toward Kentucky, "the Kentuckian" became again John Green Hanning. The resumption of his own name made him feel better, and he needed something to make him feel better, for he did not actually feel well. After the days on the wide open range, the train seemed narrow, stuffy, and dirty. His new city clothes seemed determined to choke him. They were too tight across the shoulders and too loose at the wrists; the coat seemed entirely superfluous and the trousers were awkward and stiff; the new tan shoes felt like unbendable boards. All in all, John was most uncomfortable, and the only thing right about the whole situation was the direction that the train was going. John was going home and that made all the unbearables bearable.

At Nashville, Tennessee, he was very glad to leave the train. He would have preferred two nights in the saddle to one hour on the Pullman seat, but now it was over. He was up from the Rio Grande and nearing old Kentucky. Without any delay in the "big city," he took the stagecoach for Owensboro. This may have been more bumpy than the train, but it was not so smoky, and now John was passing through familiar territory. His curiosity to note any changes and his satisfaction to recognize old homesteads and plantations, his rejuvenation as he passed spots that called up many a prank and many a happening, all made the long ride seem short and the jolting pass unnoticed.

A few miles outside Owensboro, he was surprised to find himself getting excited. He, the cowboy from down by the Rio Grande, was actually getting nervous. Now that the moment was nearing when he would have to face the folks, he was losing his usual assurance. The past nine years dropped from him like an hour, and he felt as small and as ashamed as when he had awakened under a tree to find that he had "gotten even" with his father, but that he was an exile. It seemed but yesterday that he had glared at his dad and grown sullen. It seemed but last night that he had stolen out into the darkness to send the harvest of a year up in flame and smoke. He was almost wishing that he had not come back, but before he could think what to do, he was deposited at the corner of the road that led to home, and the stage was driving off. With a shrug of his shoulders, very reminiscent of the shrug he had given nine years before, one that was half resignation and half desperation, he turned and stepped out the last stretch that would bring him home.

His heart beat faster as he came in view of the house. He took it all in at a glance. Nothing had changed. Everything was as orderly and as quiet as ever, even to the dog sleeping on the front steps. At last he turned in off the road and headed for the front door. His heart was pounding now. Who would be the first to meet him? What would they say? What would he say? Just before he got to the porch, the old dog stirred, pricked up his ears, sniffed, and barked. It was a joyous bark, and with it he was off the porch in a flash. Two bounds brought him to his old master. Then, leaping up on his hind legs, he placed his two front paws on John Green Hanning's chest. "Down, boy! Down! Quiet, old fellow. Quiet!" But it was too late. The joyous barking had brought a little lady to the window. She gave one look and ran to the front door.

She opened it and for a second stood still, looking at this lean, leather-skinned, easy-walking man who had just come onto the porch. Then her arms went out and without a single word mother and son enfolded one another in a happy embrace. At last John laughed through his tears and said, "Come, Mother, let me see you smile. Your firebug is home again."

With that she placed her hands on his shoulders, leaned back a little, and studied his face. Then she said, "No! You haven't changed a bit," and bringing down his head, she kissed him.

With arms about one another, they went into the house. They had not gone through the first room, when the back door opened and John Hanning, Sr., who had been summoned by a very excited black boy calling, "Marse Jawn's home! Marse Jawn's home!" hurried through the kitchen. Out went his right hand as he walked up to this deeply tanned and wiry looking fellow, and with the words, "My boy," father and son clasped hands. Volumes were spoken in the pressure of palms and the grip of fingers. A confession was heard, absolution given, and nine years of separation blotted out.

The Hanning household took on new life that day, and as the family was seated at supper a close observer would have noticed something. He would have noticed that John Senior looked younger, happier, more full of boyish glee than John Junior. The young Hannings were all questions, while the mother and father looked for their son's replies more avidly than did the questioners. But it was their son that they were looking at and listening to and not his replies. In every eye that rested on this prodigal, there was love; every glance was gluttonous, for that first night the Hannings could not see enough, hear enough, feel enough of this boy now become a man, who only nine years before had broken the family's heart. Love is so forgiving and so forgetful! It is very true that God has put much of his own mercy into that love which we call family love.

As for the ex-cowboy, he reveled in it all. Just as a graceful morning-glory opens wide its broad-brimmed cup to be filled with the gold of the rising sun, so did John Green Hanning expand and unfurl into full flower in the warmth of the family's affection. All the kindness in his character, all the chivalry in his soul, all the tender, gentle, and genuine affection in his heart rose to the surface; they were seen shining in his eyes, heard ringing in his words, and felt in his every touch. John Green Hanning was having a rebirth.

The wonder of his return did not wear out for months. In fact, it did not wear out at all, it was supplanted by the wonder of his rehabilitation. From down by the Rio Grande to Kentucky is a far cry, but the cowboy ways fell from young Hanning as a crystal of frost falls from a windowpane when the sun starts mounting the sky. Young John became a farmer, a tobacco farmer, and he became it in such real earnest that his father often wondered what magic of disciplining and what art of character chiseling was hidden in the life of an American cowboy who rides by the Rio Grande. Young

John was a revelation. His restlessness had gone, his carelessness and indifference had completely vanished. He was a new man—a worker with a will, an interested son who cared much for his father's holdings and much more for his father himself.

One day Mr. Hanning came upon his son as he stood eyeing the tobacco barn. For some little while he watched him, wondering what could be absorbing this boy of his. Before he could speak, however, John had turned. The boy started in surprise, gave a shadow of a smile, and then, walking up to his father, he put his two hands on his shoulders, and with a nod toward the tobacco barn, said, "Dad, I'm sorry about that, mighty sorry." Quickly the older man's arms came up and went around the shoulders of his son, and as he pressed him to his side, he said, "Forget it, boy. Forget it. That is dead!"

This is the only reference that was ever made to the affair. But even though John Green had received full and final pardon from his father, he never did forget this crime that he had committed because of his ever-present determination to "get even."

There was another confession that young John made, but this was to his mother. One evening as they sat alone and he had been describing some of the beauties of the country down by the Rio Grande, he told her that he used to sing to his horse. She laughed at such a picture—a grown man singing to a horse. John laughed too, but then he told his mother what a friend a horse can be, what intimacy grows between the man and the animal, and what affection is mutually expressed.

"John, you're sentimental," said his mother.

"No, Mother," said John. "I'm appreciative."

"Well, what sort of songs did you sing to your horse?" asked the bewildered but delighted mother.

"Oh, all sorts," said John. "You know the cowboys have their own songs, a whole lot of them. But do you know, Mother, in my last years down there, I wasn't singing cowboy songs at all. I was always singing the songs of the South. Know why? I was homesick, and I didn't know it. Gosh, Mother, it's great to be home again!" Then quite paradoxically, he broke into a rollicking song of the plain.

Song seemed to have taken hold of the Hanning homestead. The little mother sewed, dusted, and tidied up with a happy song on her lips; Mr. Hanning was whistling or humming all the day long; while from barn and from field, from carriage shed and house, the clear, sweet voice of John Junior was ever issuing. Not only was the day made brilliant with song, but the purple and gold of the sunset and the dark of the approaching dusk along with the silver witchery of the night were made more mellow and more enchanting by the velvety silver of a tenor voice. His voice could conjure up vistas of faraway places, caress you with the love in a mother's lullaby, or set your pulses pounding with the rich world of feeling that is hidden in the heart of a Negro spiritual. John Green Hanning could sing! Sing as very few mortals can sing.

Though the youngsters of the family continually pestered him for songs of the prairie and the plain, John never refused. When his sisters could not accompany him on the piano, he would take up his guitar and set old Kentucky's air ringing with cowboy yodels and serenades. John loved to use his voice of velvet and never tired of singing for his family.

But John still had his temper. Horses, mules, and men knew that. He was controlled and contained with the family and while around the house, but at work, in his dealings with men and while in the fields, he was still the same old volcano, ready to erupt in the flash of a second, and the lava emitted was as hot and as searing as that of yesteryear. Truth to tell, John's temper was bridled, but it was far from broken.

Yes, John Green Hanning gave much happiness to those whom he had hurt, as he showed a deep respect and manly affection for his father, a boy's love and devotion toward his mother, and a big brother chivalry toward his sisters. But one black cloud marred the beauty of a summer's sky. It appeared on the first Sunday after his return. It was Mass time. The girls of the family were putting their finishing touches to their "Sunday best." The mother was quietly waiting for them, while the father, with a lot of good-natured banter about the pride of women in their Sunday clothes, was urging them to hurry. Then it happened. John Green startled them all by announcing that he was not going to church.

Good-natured banter ceased. The girls continued their primping, but in silence and with nervous fingers. The father, in a puzzled and somewhat frightened tone, asked why, only to hear that he had lost his faith, had given up his God and no longer believed the truths of the Roman Catholic Church.

The air became electric. Sisters and brothers became silent. Father just stared. But Mother choked out a tear-filled, "John, dear, won't you please come, just to satisfy me? It's a long time, you know, since I had you at my side in public. Please come." She won. Sin-filled John Green's soul undoubtedly was, but it was not dead to chivalry, and through the tear-filled voice of a mother, God accomplished what he had failed to achieve through divine command.

John Green Hanning went to church that Sunday and every Sunday thereafter, but John Green Hanning did not take part in the Mass. Through unbelieving eyes he watched the moving miracle of miracles. The prodigal had returned to his earthly home, but he was still far from the embrace of his heavenly Father. In his heart there was rebellious denial and he showed it in his action as he sneeringly sat through the most solemn moments of the sacrifice.

But we have touched the depths; from now on we slowly ascend. The sneerer at the sacrifice will yet become the lover of the Slain. This ingrate will yet show you how to be grateful; he will show you how God works and how you are to work with and for God.

John was not up from the Rio Grande very long when something new came into his life—something that had its share in the refining process. He had not been home a year when he began to sing not only *for* somebody else but *to* somebody else. Not all of his evenings were spent on the front porch or in the front room of his own home. There were certain days when John would very carefully wash up after the day's work, change into his "Sunday best," and with a sheepish grin to his father and the trace of a boyish blush to his mother, would set off down the road humming some sweet little tune. Her name was Mary, and she was Catholic.

I will not say that John Hanning fell in love; at least, not madly in love, even though most of the things that this boy did were madly done. But he was greatly attracted to and by Mary. This was something entirely new to John. Unquestionably he did not and could not fully analyze the feeling of completeness and content that he found in Mary's company. He did not know that he was tasting the fullness of the spirit, that he was enjoying his psychological complement. Feminine mind, feminine heart, and feminine ways he had encountered in his mother and his sisters, but Mary was different, entirely different. She made him mad often, and puzzled him almost always. Yet, he felt bigger, better, happier in her company than he had ever felt before. Just why it was so, he never asked himself. He knew that it was so, and that sufficed.

In the beginning it was only on formal occasions that he met this girl. If you had told him that he was seeking her out, he would have resented it. Nevertheless, when young people gathered and when young people danced, you could always find John looking for Mary. His mother enjoyed many a chuckle, as her son would say, "I'm going with the boys tonight, Ma." She knew that he meant it. She knew that he was going with the boys all right, but she also knew that there would be as many girls there as boys; he was going with Mary. The mother rejoiced, for she knew that Mary was working on the soul of her son as well as on his heart. Mary was a staunch Catholic, and staunch Catholic girls make courtship a convert class! Mother would pray—let Mary do the talking. And Mary very wisely did. She announced as a matter of course that John would accompany her to church whenever she went—and John did!

Things went on this way for the better part of two years, and John Green Hanning never knew why he felt so full of life and energy at sundown on certain days of the week; why he sang with more abandon and a deeper, newer tenderness; why he more and more frequently said, "I'm going with the boys tonight, Ma." Then one day his father met him as he made his morning round of inspection, and said to him, "John, you're not getting any younger."

"No, I'm not," came the reply, but with a lift to the voice that made the statement a question.

"At your age I was a married man, father of a little family."

"Yes," came the puzzled rejoinder.

"Mary's a fine girl, John."

"Uh-huh," grunted John. He started to play with his horse's mane and stopped looking directly at his father.

HIS OLD KENTUCKY HOME

The father waited some time and patted the neck of his own horse, but finally broke the heavy silence that had fallen with, "Why don't you settle down, John? I'm getting old and you're not getting any younger."

"Ah, tush! What are you talking about? Getting old. Why, you're a young man yet," came the speedy reply.

"All right, son. I just thought I'd tell you. No harm meant. I don't want to interfere in your business, but I do say again that Mary's a fine girl and that you are not getting any younger. Think it over, boy." And with that he turned his horse's head and went riding off to another part of the farm.

That very night John "popped the question," not very gracefully, not very gallantly, not at all gently. In fact, "popped" is not the right word, "blurted the question" would be more truly descriptive of what actually took place. For John was nervous, John was mad, John was very self-conscious.

However, Mary knew her man and, though it almost choked her, she said, "Why, John, this is so sudden." She knew that it was the conventional reply, but what was almost choking her was the fact that for once the conventional reply was literally true. John had been sudden, most sudden. Be that as it may, they became engaged, seriously engaged, and John came home that night not ecstatically happy, but greatly relieved...it was over!

Engagements in those days were not only serious affairs; they were sacred. Of course, the people of the early eighties did not have our enlightenment, nor our speed in execution. They were so backward, so positively medieval as to think that 11:45 p.m. was late and that a couple should be engaged for at least six months before they thought of marriage. They had a lot of strange and, as many moderns say, stupid customs and queer ways of looking at things. For instance, John was engaged to Mary and yet he did not see her every night in the week nor spend the entire weekend with her, and when he did see her, even on those gala nights of a barn dance, he always left her near midnight, and never after it. Think of it! She was his "intended" and he, her "to be," yet they never allowed nor were allowed any more intimacies than the hurried, shy and always pure "goodnight kiss." Weren't they strange people—these Catholic couples of the early eighties!

Of course, this pair, John and Mary, were only country yokels. They lived near the little town of Owensboro, Kentucky, an out-of-the-way place. Hence, not too much is to be expected from them. Their "I.Q." would never compare with the "I.Q." of the city-bred twentieth-century couples. And yet, this simple pair with their backwoods ways, this pair who believed in long engagements and short nights of company keeping, rather than in long nights and early mornings of courting with short engagements and speedy marriages, happened to be in perfect accord with the principles enunciated by the wisest woman in the world, the holiest woman in the world, the oldest and the most experienced woman in the world...holy Mother Church!

The Last Man in the World

John's mental modes for the first few weeks after he had become engaged would have fascinated any psychoanalyst. He was happy and distressed, content and upset; he felt that life was over and that life had just begun; he hated to go to work and could not find enough to do; he wanted time to think, to plan, to ponder, and he wished that he could stop thinking. He felt that he could not see enough of Mary and that he had seen her altogether too much. He was delighted to think himself a man engaged, and yet he would often be irked with himself for ever having "blurted the question." All of which is but another way of saying that perhaps for the first in all his thirty years, John Green Hanning was looking life full in the face and was startled by the vision.

Yes, John was startled by the vision; in fact, he was somewhat frightened by it. Here he was in middle age, and yet he had never come face to face with the what, the why and the wherefore of his own personal, individual existence.

Oh, he knew the catechism answers. He knew that "he was made by God," and that "he was made to know him, to love him, and to serve him in this world and so to be happy with him in the next." Yes, John knew these answers, but that is all that they had ever been to him, just "catechism answers." They had never become dynamic, driving forces; they had never become vivid, vital principles of life. They had remained just words that one must learn; they had never become truths that one must live.

He had learned the answers and learned them well, but they were only items of memory; they had never become the illumination for his mind, the inspiration for his will, the affection for his heart that would have made them grace. They were only words that had gone into his head; they were not grace that had gone down into his heart. These answers about the whence, the why and the wherefore of life—these answers that are the golden epitome of all the world's philosophies and nuggets of divine truth—had made as much impression on the soul of our hero as quicksilver makes when it runs over a highly polished surface. Like most of us, John had learned these answers to get a high mark in the teacher's book, never realizing that by living them he would be earning the highest mark in the book of life.

Perhaps the fault was not all his. Perhaps he had teachers such as most of us have had: teachers who can make history, geography, and arithmetic live, teachers who can dramatize even the multiplication table, but who make the "catechism hour" a class without life or lyricism, an hour devoid of all imagery and emotion, a mere memory lesson. Perhaps John's teachers made 1492 and 1776 live again for the avid mind of youth, but did nothing about the drama of creation and that greater drama of redemption. Perhaps they forgot that the discovery of America and the Declaration of Independence are far less important to us than what happened in paradise after time began and what took place in Palestine from A.D. 27 to 30. As if it were more important for us to know the addition and subtraction of numbers, than to know that a human nature added to the divine nature by the Second Person subtracted the infinite debt that man owed to God! As if a child should be carefully taught the cancellation of arbitrary signs and symbols, and not much more carefully taught the cancellation of sins! As if the mind of youth, just as it opens into flower, should be made acquainted with all the wars of the world and all the world wars and not more thoroughly acquainted with the never-ending war of man with Satan and sin! As if it were more important for man to know the cause of the downfall of Greece and Rome than to know that his own worst enemy is a domestic one...himself!

Education, to be real, must be synonymous with edification—upbuilding. Its whole purpose must be to "bring out" and to "build up" the man that is buried in the boy, and build him up to the gigantic stature of Jesus Christ. Secular education is not and cannot be true education, because a person can never be educated unless he is "brought out" and led to God. The modern public school system, from kindergarten to state university, may teach a person how to make a living but it will never teach him how to make a life, and until a person knows how to make a life, he is not educated.

Please understand me! I know that our schools and colleges are wonderlands of marvel and mystery. It is a good thing to have gone through them; for it is a very good thing to know about physical and chemical changes; but it is much better to know about transubstantiation, for that is higher than any physical and chemical change; that is a miracle. It is a good thing to study biology and go in for physical hygiene, but it is far better to study what biology cannot teach—the birth of our God from a Virgin—and to go in for spiritual hygiene. It is a good thing to have studied the humanities, but it would have been far better to have studied the divinity. To know the epics and the sagas of literature is a grand thing, but the saga of all sagas is that of the human family, and that is not taught in our learned literary circles; and the greatest of all epics—those of creation and redemption—are either unknown or ignored. Secular education teaches about the stars and the planets, and that is a good thing; but it does not teach about "our home beyond the stars" and about the maker of the planets, and that is a very bad thing! For the first without the second might be knowledge, the first with the second is wisdom! Until we aim at this wisdom in all our teachings, we will ever be the "blind leading the blind"—and that combination never has a happy ending.

It is the religion text that is the golden book of the world's sublimest wisdom; it is the only true dream maker and character builder; for it is the textbook of all textbooks, man's very guide to God. But religion must be taught with enthusiasm!

Perhaps John Hanning's teachers are more to blame than John for the fact that he was in his early thirties before he looked life full in the face and asked himself, "What is it all about?" and "Where am I going?" His engagement to Mary shook him loose from the habit most of us contract of just drifting through life, going on from day to day, rutted in the deep rut of custom, convention, and routine, and never asking ourselves "Where to?" "Where from?" and "Why?"

John suddenly realized that he was about to cast his life into a very definite mold, that he was about to take one of those few steps that can be rightly called irrevocable. He knew that he was about to do one of the most serious and sacred things of his life, and this made him pause. At times he was glad that his dad had spoken to him in the fields that morning and advised him to "think it over." At times he was very glad that he had mustered up enough courage to blurt out his "Will you?" At such times as these the only regret he knew was that he had waited so long. But there were other times when he did not feel so happy, nor so perfectly at ease. These were the times when he would try to puzzle out what looked to him like the smile of the sphinx on the face of life. What *was* it all about and where was *he* going?

On the night of his proposal, Mary had stated that "her man" must be a real Catholic, and had casually added that going to church on Sunday did not make a real Catholic. John had squirmed under the statement, for he did not know just how much Mary had heard about his attitude during Mass, nor was he at all sure of just what she meant by her words. Still he answered with a noncommittal, "I understand," even though he well knew that he did not understand, that he was far from understanding what she knew and what she meant, and this obscurity worried him. This obscurity worried him, but like a true Southerner he felt himself bound to every implication in his answer to a question of whose full import he was not sure.

The God of love is never beaten! Somehow, sometime, someplace or through some person he finds a way of stretching out his hand to the boldest, brazenest, blindest, and most defiant. To John Green Hanning he reached out through the eyes of his mother, the patience of his family, and the statement of his fiancée—and first of all through the eyes of his mother.

Mary Jane Hanning was a Catholic mother. When I have said that, I have said all that one can say and I have paid the highest tribute possible to a woman. Genius stutters when it tries to speak of motherhood; who then can essay a tribute to the glory of all motherhood— Catholic motherhood? Language is often found weak and wanting; here it is futile. So again I say that Mary Jane Hanning was a Catholic mother and with that I rest. She was not going to argue with this boy of hers. She had asked him to come to Sunday Mass. He had come. The rest she would entrust to God. She knew the story of St. Monica. She knew how that fond mother had prayed and wept and followed her sinning son from Africa even to Milan; and she knew that she had done this not because she was a saint, but because she was Augustine's mother! Mary Jane Hanning prayed. If she wept, she did it in secret. Tears and prayers were for God, for her son she had only eloquent eyes.

Sunday morning was a torture for our prodigal. And yet, he would not give in. What used to tear his very soul was the eloquence in the eyes of his mother. She never spoke. She only looked and smiled. A brave smile it was, but her son looked deep into those smiling eyes and saw that his mother was begging even as her heart was breaking. He never forgot those eyes, and so God's grace of conversion and repentance came through the demand of his fiancée and the loving patience of his family, but especially through the eloquent eyes of his mother. Yet, sad to tell, John cooperated with that grace only after those eyes were closed forever.

In 1882 the world grew very lonely for John Green Hanning, despite his family, his friends and his bride-to-be. In 1882 he felt more lonely than he had ever felt down by the Rio Grande, for in this year his mother died. Then it was that the man became a boy and the memories that flooded his mind drained his heart. Echoes from the forgotten years rang through his being and the silent Hanning home was filled with his absent mother's words. John Green wept at this parting—wept bitter tears, tears that came from the depths of his soul, tears that wrung his very heart, and the loneliness of a newly mounded grave made him think long, long thoughts about life, about heaven and about God.

When the first fury of his grief was spent, John Green Hanning did the thing that his mother had prayed for, wept for, lived for and, perhaps, died for—John Green Hanning prayed. He prayed more earnestly than he had prayed since childhood, prayed more with his heart and soul than he had ever prayed before, prayed with tears in his eyes, tears in his heart and tears on his tongue. God was not distant these days. God was near, very near, and he was made to listen to a heartbroken boy, who had the years and the form of a man but the lonely heart of a child. He was made to listen to heartbroken pleas and prayers for the soul of that saint of all dear saints, John's mother. It was then that God also listened to some contrition and to some heartfelt thanks for having brought a renegade up from the Rio Grande and a runaway back to his mother for the last three years of her life. Yes, his mother's death made John Green Hanning think true thoughts about life, about heaven and about God; it made him study closely just where he was going. Love had leaped the grave; and a mother, after death, accomplished what she had failed to achieve in life—the conversion of her boy!

Naturally, this heartbreak outlawed all thoughts of a wedding for a year and for more than a year. This loss drove John closer to Mary and yet, by one of those strange qualms of conscience, which you know is wrong, but which you love to find in a man, kept him further from her. John Green Hanning was not going to place another woman in the heart that had been so long held by his mother.

The years went on and with them went some of the fierceness from this false fear that he would or could prove untrue to his mother. Mary still wore his ring and had gotten John to sing again, but our hero was not fully recovered from the shock of what he had known was inevitable but surprised him when it came. His mother's death was a turning point in the life of John Green Hanning, for it made him return to God and look beyond time's near horizon and far beyond this world's cramped space. It made him very pointedly ask just what is life and what was he doing with it.

While he was trying to give a satisfying answer to these questions, he visited his Alma Mater. But the school did not interest him so much as the monastery, and the monastery not nearly so much as the monks. By one of those odd comparisons which we all like to make,

John contrasted himself, about to be married, with these men who would never be married. While chuckling to himself at the oddness of the contrast, it suddenly flashed on him that the world would congratulate him, wish him well, and then promptly forget him; but that the world would ever hold in awe and reverence these silent men of Gethsemani's Abbey, and in this spirit of reverential awe would call them "heroic" and "great."

This all came to John in a flash, but it lingered. He, too, felt an admiration for them—vague, misty, grudging, but it was there. It was only a twilight glimpse, yet John saw clearly enough that they had something different and had done something different, and that they were something different. Then his old longing came back. Twenty years before he had wanted to be one of them. The same longing now surged in his soul and John resented it. He wanted to be entirely rid of it. He angrily told himself that these men were misfits, strange people, odd characters who had chosen a mighty odd life. He told himself many things of like nature about these brown-and-white-robed Trappists, but he could not tell himself that they were not "great," and that made him all the more angry.

He left Gethsemani in a huff. All the way back to Owensboro, he was trying to puzzle out why he thought so much of these men and yet so little of them. What was it that made him think of them as heroes and yet as half-wits? Before he had reached home, he had settled it this way: they were heroes because they were living for God; they seemed half-wits because they were not living as men. It was not too clear, but it was definite enough to allow him to dismiss the matter for the time being.

That night at the supper table, however, he brought it up again. Perhaps he was hoping to hear his father rant as of old and thus confirm him in his stand of "hero and half-wit." He asked his dad just what he thought of the Trappist monks, and thus started a series of exclamations that rendered him speechless. His father simply said, "marvelous men." His brothers were equally as brief and equally as eulogistic. But his sisters had much to say about "saints" and "angels of the earth" and "God's chosen few." Even the youngest Hanning, Cora, whom John loved the best of all his sisters, had her "oh's" and "ah's" about holiness and happiness and saving one's soul. By the time the last brief tribute had been paid, John did not dare to breathe his thoughts about misfits, strange people and odd characters. He gave a noncommittal, "Uh-huh" and changed the subject.

For weeks he could not get the thought of Gethsemani's monks out of his mind. At the strangest moments and in the oddest places they would rise before him. When riding about the farm, supervising the hired hands, he would think, "That is what the monks do"; when going to church on Sundays he would think, "This is all the monks do"; and even when he was with Mary, the men of Gethsemani would come into his mind, for walking with her he would think, "This is what the monks do not do."

One bright day as he was watching his men cultivate the tobacco plants, the monks again came into his mind. In something of a fury he wheeled his horse around, and with a savage, "Damn the monks! Why are they always on my mind?" he set his startled mount to a mad gallop. After a wild ride he came to a wood. Here he reined in his panting steed, slid from the saddle, threw the rein over the horse's head, and sat down with his back against a tree, saying, "I'm going to settle this thing once and for all." Then he began to think. Once again it was the fretful, fuming circle of: "They're great. They're good. They're strange. They're odd. But they are great and they are good. Yes, but they are strange and they are odd." Round and round and round he went, until suddenly he thought: "Gosh! Anyone can marry a girl, but not anyone can be a monk." Then after some time he said aloud, "I wanted to be a monk long before I ever wanted to marry, anyhow."

This sobered him. He calmed down and admitted to himself that monks were different from the usual run of men, and the difference was that which lies between the ordinary and the extraordinary, between the good and the great. That was why people admired them so. No one would admire a man about to be married, for almost every man did that. But there was no one who would not admire a man about to become a monk, for only a very few ever did that.

This little bit of rationalization acted upon John as a revelation and inspiration. Everyone wants to be great. Everyone wants to be admired. Everyone wants to be a hero. Human beings are conceited and nothing appeals to them more than applause. That is why people become everything from flagpole sitters to trans-Atlantic flyers, from tap dancers to soapbox orators. Shakespeare has said something about man strutting his brief hour upon the stage, but what Shakespeare failed to add was that man would not enjoy his strut unless there was an applauding audience out there in the pit. This greed for glory, which is in the heart of every child of Adam, makes not only great persons but also gangsters—for if one cannot become famous, he at least can become infamous; and if the papers will not praise, they will censure. And some care not whether it be eulogy, raillery, or pillory; they are

THE LAST MAN IN THE WORLD 87

happy as long as their names are in print.

This tendency explains what happened in the head and heart of John Green Hanning. The last man in the world that you or I would ever suspect of wishing to become a contemplative monk is this same J. G. Hanning. Yet the idea was conceived and the ambition harbored by this last man in the world, and all because of that urge in the soul to be different, to be great, to win applause and gain renown. As he sat in the shade of a towering tree and watched his horse nibbling grass, this fiery Southerner seriously thought of becoming a Trappist lay brother, and though he never clearly analyzed why, one of the chief reasons was—so as to be great.

It was a much quieter man who remounted his horse and headed for home. All that day he toyed with the thought of the greatness of the Trappist monks. That night John saw Mary. To make conversation she asked him what he had been doing all day and was given the reply:

"Working and thinking."

Quite coquettishly came the question, "Of whom were you thinking?" for Mary was a woman and a woman engaged. It was the normal question and, of course, she expected the normal reply. But what she heard was far from normal.

"I was thinking about myself," said John,

"and I was very seriously thinking about becoming a Trappist lay brother."

"A what?" gasped Mary, and then she began to laugh. Mary would have been piqued because John had not given the expected, "I was thinking of you, my dear," but the entirely unexpected reply so took her by surprise and struck her as so funny that she laughed and laughed.

"What are you laughing at?" asked John. He was getting mad.

"At you," she gulped and went on laughing.

"What's so funny about me?" John was more than mad now, he was furious.

"You—a Trappist lay brother! You—with your temper and your tongue! John, are you sober? Let me smell your breath."

But she did not smell his breath, for John had become so ragingly mad that he had stamped off muttering, "Oh, why can't a man hit a girl?"

The next morning John was cool and perfectly sober. As he went his round of morning work, he often chuckled to himself, for he was reviewing the scene he had had with Mary and it now appeared most comical even to himself. He got a great laugh not only out of the idea of having entertained the notion of becoming a Trappist, but of broaching it to the very girl he was engaged to marry. And what especially tickled him this morning was the memory of his walking off muttering to himself. He chuckled and chuckled and not infrequently laughed out loud, for he was thinking how right Mary had been and what a mad monk he would make. This was typical of John—quick to anger, quick to cool, and wise enough to laugh at himself.

He made up with Mary immediately, and as he settled into the old rut of working, eating, sleeping, singing and seeing Mary, he thought he had rid himself forever of the wild notion of joining the silent monks. For some little time he did forget it, but when it came time to set a definite date for the wedding, the urge came back to him with a newer and fiercer force. All he could see was the glamor and the greatness of doing something different, of being something different, of winning the approval and the applause of others as he gave something to God. This last element was there, was strongly there, but it was far from the dominant element. Dimly he perceived that there was something more to the Trappist life than winning the applause of others. He had a twilight glimpse of the fact that the greatness of the life came from its divine element, and that a monk does give something to God; but it was not this that moved him most. Actually, the thing that moved him most to think of Gethsemani was the thing that should have made him think of it least—it was his temper. When he recalled Mary's laugh and reflected that people in general thought that he could never lead the Trappist life, he got mad, mad enough to say, "If I weren't engaged, I'd show them!" and very shortly this changed to, "Even if I am engaged, I'll show them!"

It was a very muddled affair in his own mind. He wanted to be called great and he really wanted to be great. He wanted to save his soul and he wanted to show people. He wanted to give something to God and he wanted to be different. Varied indeed were the motives and varied the ideals, but ever and always as he fought out the battle in his own mind, the conviction kept growing that he should be a monk. The longing of the years came back and the words of his confessor and friend, who did not command but who often advised that he give it serious thought, were having their effect.

John was temperamental as we have already seen, but he was never more so than during these months, as he battled a vocation and struggled with the call of the world. He was very temperamental, but the accent was not entirely on the "temper"; quite a bit of the stress was on the "mental," for while he flew into a rage often these days, he also did some stiff and very sober thinking. At long last he determined to tell Mary that the urge was on him again, and that, if she would give him his freedom, he would go to Gethsemani.

With John, to plan was to act. As soon as he saw Mary, he said very quickly and very bluntly, "Mary, I've been thinking again of becoming a monk. If you give me permission, I'll go to the monastery and try the life."

This time Mary did not laugh. She started, then looked away. After toying with a button on her dress as she looked off into space, she very quietly asked, "Have you given this serious thought, John?"

"Very," was the quick reply. "And, Mary, I'm convinced that I should give it a try."

Again silence fell. A long silence during which John grew nervous, but he did not grow mad. Finally the words came—slow words, sad words. "You may go, John..." Then, with a new timber and a new tone, she added, "But if you do..." There followed a pause during which John kept shifting from foot to foot. "But if you do..." she repeated in a higher pitch, "don't let me ever see your face again. For I wouldn't marry an ex-monk, no!" and with added intensity, "not even if he were the last man in the world!"

Here her voice broke, and with it her control. Mary turned on her heel and flew into the house, for she was not going to cry in front of the man she had almost married.

John, too, turned on his heel, but much more slowly. Then with leaden feet he started to walk home. His heart was heavier that night than it had been since he was twenty-one. He wanted to be a Trappist, but he did not want to break people's hearts in order to be one. Every step of the way home was a battle. Often he half turned, ready to tell Mary that it was all a bad dream; for John Green Hanning, with all his fiery temper, had a heart as sensitive and as soft as wax.

Breaking the news to the family was a very different affair. Mouths flew open, eyes flew open, and all caught their breath, for they, too, thought that John was the last man in the world who would think of the life of a Trappist lay brother. When he was fifteen they had more or less expected it, but now at thirty-six...no wonder they grew exclamatory.

When John got to the quiet of his room and weighed their exclamations, he grew angry. He saw why people looked aghast when he spoke of Gethsemani. They thought that he could not do it, could not hold his temper or his tongue, could not be a quiet monk. So that was it, was it? Then in a fit of temper John voiced in no quiet way his determination, "Well, I'll show them! I'll show them what I can do!" And with this fire he set off for the monastery.

Are you amazed at the motives that led John Green Hanning to the Trappists? Are you appalled that a vocation should come through vindictiveness, greed for glory, desire for greatness and hunger for approval and applause? Did I shock you by bas-reliefing the natural and touching the supernatural with a light and cursory hand? If I did, I am happy and hasten to press my advantage, for I want you to know that there is such a thing as a salutary selfishness and a praiseworthy pride.

Jesus Christ called twelve to his side personally and the thirteenth he struck from his horse; but for the nineteen hundred years since then, every vocation that I know of has been the most natural of supernatural works. No longer does Christ appear personally. No longer does he strike people from their horses. But he calls thousands and thousands to his side by working in, on and through their natures. Just as he worked in Palestine, so does he work today. Do you remember how he appealed to Peter and Andrew, James and John, who were fishermen? He said to them, "Come, and I will make you fishers of men." Have you never known why the twelve were so attached to him? They wanted to be great, so great that they were even squabbling as to who was going to be the greatest. Do you not recall how James and John played on his sympathies? That is an intensely natural and human story. These "sons of thunder" were so greedy for the glory of being first in his kingdom that they got their mother to plead for them. They knew the sensitive heart of their master, so they played on it, and played on it with the most delicate of instruments—the tenderness of a mother's prayer. Yes, every apostle of Christ was drawn to the supernatural by the natural, and every follower of Christ, if he is to be a real follower of Christ, must want to be great, must be greedy for glory, must be a self-seeker; for there is a selfishness that is salutary and a pride that is praiseworthy.

Despite what certain books say, which are rhapsodies and romances rather than revelations and biographies, every vocation is ultimately founded on that salutary selfishness by which an individual, despite the whole wide world, seeks to save his own immortal soul. Every vocation has been followed because those who were called really wanted to be great. Nature and the natural are never to be despised. On them is built the supernatural!

There are spiritual writers whose books inculcate the opposite doctrine, but while they may be good writers, they are not writers of good spirituality. They show but one side of the picture and it is not the bright and the beautiful side. They would have you believe that your body is base and vile, nothing better than filth for flies and carrion for crows; but you know that it is God's glorious masterpiece, the one and only temple of your soul, the lone instrument an infinitely wise God has given you as your personal property with which to work your way to heaven. These writers are more Manichaean than Christian, for while they remember that by the body a person sins, they seem to forget that it is by the body that a person is sanctified. It is true that the body can lead one to degradation, but it is equally true that it is the only personal and proper means for one's exaltation and glorification. Without your body your soul cannot be saved. These pessimists are forever moaning complaints in a minor key, while real Christian writers are always giving voice to a glorious *magnificat* in the full burst of a magnificent major.

Your senses, your passions, your impulses and your instincts are all good, grand, glorious possessions; for they all come from God. Your senses are to be guarded, not despised. They are your gateways to glory, for without them you could never have an idea, without an idea you could never have will-action, and without will-action you can never have merit, and without merit you can never see God! Your passions, too, are glorious gifts. They are to be properly directed, not destroyed. If they riot, they can lead you to hell; but if you regulate them, they will give you a passionate love for Jesus Christ, and that, you know, is sanctity. Instincts and impulses can be dangers; they are also your greatest helps, for your deepest instinct is an instinct for God and your most ready impulse is an impulse for greatness and glory.

Laugh then, if you will, at these patrons of the partial view, but do not take them as your guides, no matter how many abbreviations are stamped after their names. For myself, I enjoy the mental magic by which a person can seriously consider himself a "worm of the earth," even while he is ambitioning to become "like unto God." Just remember that our nature is a fallen nature but not foul; it is weak but not vile; it is wounded but not wretched. Because it is damaged is no reason that it should be destroyed. Hold fast to the fact that nature comes from God, and that when God wanted to work his miracle of miracles and his greatest work of love, he assumed a human nature!

It is a good thing to know our limitations, but not unless we also know our potentialities. For while a "superiority complex" is disgusting, a deadly and dangerous thing, it is not nearly so dangerous or so deadly as an "inferiority complex" where things spiritual are concerned. We must become divine, and the only foundation on which we can build is what so many writers decry...our human natures. They call it humility to consider oneself lower than the earthworm and to revile one's body. But that is not humility, that is "humbug." Half-truths are always more dangerous than whole lies, and the lopsided view of human nature taken by some writers is at best a half-truth. They have forgotten their human psychology, much of their logic, and all of their life in Christ. He always worked on, in and through human nature; and today, with his gifts of grace, he works the same way.

John Green Hanning went to Gethsemani because he was selfish, proud and vindictive. He wanted to save his soul, to be great and to show people that he could be different. He proved it—proved it to the hilt and had all friends, enemies and ordinary acquaintances saying, "Well, of all the people who would or could do such a thing, I thought John Green Hanning was the last man in the world!"

The Irresistible and the Immovable Meet

There are many days that I would love to have lived; many men and many minds I would long to have known; many scenes I would wish to have witnessed. Perhaps one of heaven's joys will be the ability to recreate, recapture, and re-enact the past. If so, then I will have the life of Christ—all but Calvary—relived. I will see his miracles, hear his sermon on the mount, and listen to his parables by the sea. Then I will search the minds of men: the minds of Plato, Socrates and Aristotle; I long to scrutinize the creative genius of Homer, Virgil, Euripides, Sophocles and Aeschylus; I want to feel the pulse of an Alexander, a Caesar, a Napoleon and a Washington. There are millions of intimate things that I want to know, and heaven alone can give them...the men, their minds and their moods. And if heaven is going to be heaven, it must give me the day that John Green Hanning and Dom Benedict Berger faced each other, and John asked to be admitted as a lay brother in the community of Gethsemani's Abbey. For on that day an almost irresistible force met an almost immovable object.

It was June 4, 1885; the place, Gethsemani's cold, monastic parlor; the time, mid-afternoon. These things we know, but we do not know what went on in the minds of these two men as they faced each other for the first time with the prospect and possibility of assuming the spiritual relationship of father and son. Dom Benedict undoubtedly thought of this relationship. John Green most likely merely looked upon the abbot as a possible "boss."

Judged by any standard, Dom Benedict Berger was a hard man. Exteriorly he had the commanding features of a Caesar, interiorly he had all the rigor of the monks of the Thebaid. He was abbot of a community of "Cistercians of the Strict Observance" and knew but one law and one life, and that was to live the Rule of St. Benedict to the letter. He did it himself, and he expected, yes, demanded that every man under him do the same. He was stern, strict, severe and hard, but never harsh.

At any rate, you can imagine the spiritual energies that met that day, as two hands clasped and two pairs of eyes engaged each other in that quick flash of immediate appraisement. The abbot was the incarnation of regulated and inflexible will power; John Green, the embodiment of undisciplined but fierce determination. Two mighty forces met that afternoon; Dom Benedict admitted John Hanning and John Hanning accepted Dom Benedict. But neither had the vaguest notion of the tremendous task they were taking upon themselves as one asked, "May I come in?" and the other answered, "You may." If either saw what price he would have to pay to live with the other for the next few years, yet still entered into the contract, then a miracle took place on that June 4.

John was admitted and there followed a series of revelations that truly amazed the ex-cowboy. Despite his thirty-six years of existence, John experienced a touch of nervousness as he began to lead the Trappist life. Everyone had told him how hard it was, and he himself had slightly feared the severity of silence, abstinence, work and prayer. However, he plunged in, and like many another who has dived into a water which for some time had frightened him, John found that once in, the water was not so cold. Anticipation is almost always worse than realization.

To continue with the same metaphor, for some weeks things went "swimmingly." John was up early, very early—in fact, earlier than he had ever been up before, for John was up at 2 a.m. But he did not mind this, for he had gone to bed earlier than he had ever gone before. A man who goes to bed just after the sun cannot feel outraged when aroused just before the sun. Then again, early rising was not entirely new to John; cowboys and farmers often meet the dawn. But what was new to John was to get up in a hurry, and in a hurry hasten to the church in order to pray. The novelty of this occurrence so surprised John that when he got to the church, he could not do what he had hurried there to do. He could not pray. But who could pray as he saw sixty-five or seventy men silently file into a huge church and quietly take their respective places? Who could pray when only seven minutes after the bell for rising had rung, the simple chant of the little office of our Lady broke the stillness of the dimly-lighted church, and spectral figures in white up near the transepts were seen to bow and rise in unison, and heard to sing in unison? Who could pray as all around him was shadow and marvel and mystery? Who could pray in an atmosphere so saturated with prayer?

But John did his best on his beads. He had been told to follow the choir religious in the opening prayers and then to say ten *Ave Maria's* for Matins and ten for Lauds. He had memorized the Latin and did as he had been told, but of all the distracted prayers that John Green Hanning had ever said, these *Ave's*, said while monks in white were chanting and brothers in brown were bending over and straightening up at certain definite intervals, were the most distracted. Just when John thought he had caught the movement, the whole thing ended. It was 2:30 and time for mental prayer.

John knelt down and prepared to do what he had never done before—to pray without using words, to pray without prayer book, beads or memorized formulas—to pray with his mind and his heart and not with his lips. He thought it was a mighty funny way to pray, but he tried it. The novelty of the method intrigued him. He very conscientiously put himself in the presence of God and made an act of faith. He followed it with an act of adoration; he then called upon the Holy Spirit to help him, and he united all his actions with the merits of Jesus Christ. He had been told to do these things. He had been told that this was the proper way to commence meditation. When he had gone thus far, he tried to picture for himself the subject of his meditation, and for many weeks this is about as far as John ever got. This picturing for himself, this making a mental representation, sometimes caused such strain that it produced sterility, while at other times the picture was pulsing with so much life that it amounted to a distraction. This mental prayer was a hazard to John. It presented the biggest difficulty of the day, because, like most beginners, he was frightened by terms and mentally shackled by method. But he worked so hard at the technique that before he ever got down to the reflections and the considerations, the time was usually up and he gave his attention to Mass.

In 1885, Holy Communion was not the daily luxury that it is in the life of a religious today. John had to satisfy himself with assistance at daily Mass. In the summer months the lay brothers' Mass was celebrated at 3 a.m., so John had the new experience of assisting at Mass in the lay brothers' choir, while the monks of the monastery chanted the canonical office in their choir up toward the transepts.

All this intense spiritual activity had John wide awake for months. The quick succession of events kept him on the alert, and he found it hard to believe that two hours could pass so quickly and so enjoyably. Before 4 a.m., John had said Matins and Lauds of the little office and of the canonical office, had made a half hour of mental prayer, had assisted at Mass, and had finished Prime of both offices, that of our Lady and that of the Church. Do you wonder that John began to think of himself as a human dynamo?

Chuckling to himself over all he had accomplished, he arranged his bed, changed his clothes and set out for the barn. The sun was just up, the grass was wet, and the air liquid with bird notes. This was as good as home, thought John, and very like home. The cows were more numerous, but they were quickly milked, for every lay brother in the community was present, and when forty-five men set to milking, a lot of cream flows into pails. This task finished, John returned to the house and partook of his very light breakfast. This was not like home, not a bit; but John did not mind; he did not have time to mind, for action was the order of the day. With a promptness that surprised him he saw all hurry to work. John joined them and spent the rest of the morning on the farm. There was a slight interruption at 9:45 a.m., during which the stipulated number of *Pater's* and *Ave's* were said for the canonical hour called Tierce. At 10:15, John came back from the fields, for the morning's work was ended.

John had often worked harder and longer. Down by the Rio Grande and at his old Kentucky home, he had often sweated more than he did at Gethsemani. No, the work did not bother John either by its nature or by its duration, for farming had been one of his avocations before he had answered his real vocation. But though the nature of the work was familiar and the hours short, there was one thing about it all that was most unfamiliar, and that was the Trappist way of working. In the years that had gone, John had seldom worked in silence. He had always been either singing or "stewing" about something; but here at Gethsemani he could not sing and, as yet, there was nothing to "stew" about. The other big difference, and this was a *big* difference, was that he was told where to work and with whom to work and how to work. But even this was not burdensome to John in the beginning, for he was most curious about the other men in the novitiate with him, and there are few better places to study a man than while he is at work.

The half hour immediately following work, John spent washing up and reading. He could never get enough time for reading, for there was a whole book of regulations that John wanted to master in a month. It is the volume of "Lay Brother Usages," and it takes the best part of two years to acquaint a novice thoroughly with its manifold details. This was the book that John wanted to finish in a month. He crammed, but the more he crammed, the more confused he became, for there are stipulations on how to walk, how to sit and how to stand, regulations on how to hold your head, your hands and your feet, rules for eating, sleeping and drinking, prescriptions for reading, writing and praying. There is nothing that a monk may do that does not have its particular directions and, of course, there are many prescriptions about what a monk may not do. John always washed up rapidly so that he could read the more fully; but even if he omitted the washing entirely, he found the time too short, and all too soon he was saying *Pater's* and *Gloria's* for the canonical hour of Sext.

At 11:00 John went to dinner, and this was the disillusionment of disillusionments. The food was plain, plain in itself and plain in its preparation. But it was plentiful. John had taken a cup of coffee and a piece of bread at 5 a.m. and had then worked in the open air for about six hours. Yet he was puzzled by the size and sharpness of his appetite. He had no meat, no fish, no eggs, but he did have plain vegetables, and he had these aplenty. Every day he found a very large serving of soup and a very large serving of a vegetable at his place. One day it would be beans, another day potatoes, a third day turnips, or carrots, or rice, or spinach, or some such green. At first John used to think that enough had been served him to do for a family, and he immediately saw that no Trappist need die of starvation. He admitted that things were not so nicely prepared as mother used to have them, and not nearly as nicely served. But he also admitted that they were as good, if not better, than what he had had down by the Rio Grande. Perhaps the sameness of the diet would have palled on John—for of all the unvarying menus that exist, the Trappist's is the most unvarying. Let Christmas, Fourth of July, or St. Bernard's feast fall on Monday, and it will make not the slightest bit of difference...beans will be served. So I say the sameness of the diet might have palled on John, were it not for the fact that he always came to the table with the sameness of appetite. He was always ready to eat.

The morning was over and by high noon John was on his bed of boards and a straw-filled mattress to take his midday rest. Often during these early days he went to the dormitory saying to himself, "Not so bad! Not so bad at all!" And he was right. Things were not so bad for John; he had fitted into the life with more ease than he or anyone else ever expected. The novelty of it all absorbed him. He had never been so completely occupied in all his years. Every moment of his day had its fixed duty, and John saw the community glide from one duty to another with all the regularity of a clock and all the smoothness of a well-oiled machine. Here was order, perfect order and perfect tranquility; here was peace. John had never lived in such a systematized atmosphere before and it intrigued him.

These first few weeks saw John alert, interested and observant. He was learning and, since all his energies were bent on acquisition, he made no effort at self-expression, and for this reason his temper was as tranquil as a summer sea. As yet John had not been crossed; hence, there were no eruptions. During these early days he was more passive than active, more intent on knowing than on showing. He was much more anxious to learn than to teach, and so his brain was more in evidence than his blood or his bile.

As I said, things were going "swimmingly." About the only thing that irked him was the "sign language." When it is necessary for Trappists to communicate an idea, they use their fingers instead of their tongues. Not as the deafmutes do with a whole alphabet, but with a very restricted vocabulary that was devised some eight hundred years ago and is supposed to cover all things that a monk need ever to "sign" about. This proved a little irritating in the beginning, for once in a while the one in charge of the novices, who may give verbal directions regarding the work, would absent himself from the place where the novices were working and then some senior novice would endeavor to show John what was to be done by using the sign language. Of course, John had not learned what we might call the ABC's of this language as yet, and the finger manipulations of the well-meaning novice either amused John or made him a little mad. He thought it all so impractical and so woodenly rigid. Surely a man would not be breaking silence if he told an ignorant postulant what to do and how to do it, thought John, but the novice thought differently and went on with his gesticulations. It often amused John to try to figure out the message the novice was aiming to convey, but there were other times when he himself was interested in the work and wanted it done rightly; then these unintelligible signs made him mad. Sometimes the fingers flashed and while John could not understand a word of it, he had to admire the novice's fluency. At other times, however, after a single sign a novice would stop, frown and look up and down, while John would smile to himself, thinking, "Either this man is a stutterer or else he's wrestling with an idea and it has thrown him."

There was much to amuse, much to interest, much to absorb, and next to nothing to irritate John these first few weeks, and that is why he usually went to his noonday rest saying, "Not so bad. Not so bad at all."

The afternoon was even more pleasant than the morning, for at 1:00 John was up and saying his office for the canonical hour of None, which was immediately followed by a brief instruction from the master of novices. How John looked forward to these instructions! Not that he was greedy for knowledge, but he was hungry, very hungry, for the sound of a human voice talking in a human way. This was the oasis in the desert of John's day. For you must remember that John had been conversing with people for over a quarter of a century. Twenty-five years is a good length of time—enough time for a habit to become fairly well rooted! That is why John enjoyed the instructions. Just as we never miss the water till the well runs dry, so John never appreciated speech until he was saturated with silence. More than likely he never knew just why he looked forward to these instructions on the rule, the customs, the catechism or the spiritual life. He may have thought that it was the information that so delighted him, but it was nothing logical that engrossed him. It was something psychological. John was not hungering for ideas, he only longed to hear human words coming from a human being, using the human voice.

John left these instructions breathing more freely. The words of the master had injected new life into him; not that they were divine, but because they were so intensely human. Every day and in every way John saw more and more that the monks were men and not mummies. If he were at home, John would have broken out into song, but he was not at home, so he went to work silently but very refreshed.

By 2:00, John was always in the fields working, and he stayed in the fields until 5:00, when a little pause was made, during which the novices gathered to say the appointed number of *Pater's* and *Gloria's* for the Vesper hour. At 5:30, the outdoor work was ended, so in single file, with some subofficial at their head, their hoe, rake or shovel under the left arm and a rosary in the right hand, the novices and postulants marched back to the house.

Sometimes John managed to say his rosary, but most of the time he was completely abstracted rather than distracted. He was completely taken out of himself and his present surroundings, as he became absorbed in that ever engrossing game of mental argumentation. John was telling himself and everyone whom he had ever known that he and they were all wrong! Yes, all wrong about this Trappist life. It was not so difficult after all. He knew that he had felt like a hero when leaving home, and people had encouraged this self-complacency by treating him as the bravest of the brave who was setting off for a war that was to be terrific. He also knew that, as he had walked down the shaded lane that leads to the monastery gate, he had felt very much the martyr, who, with unbelievable courage, was heading for the arena sands where only the strongest of the strong ever trod. Now he felt like an ordinary man living with ordinary men, leading a life that was very ordinary except for silence, abstinence and plenty of prayer. Yes, argued John, people are all wrong. This life is not so hard.

He took his supper at 6:00 with as much relish (and as much plainness) as he had taken his dinner. Then after helping the other brothers clear off the tables and wash the dishes, he had only a few moments before the entire community assembled for a fifteen- or twenty-minute reading from some recognized spiritual writer. John noticed that some of the older brothers nodded, and nodded to everything that was read. He was quite shocked at this and not a little indignant, until one warm evening he found his own eyes heavy and his own head continually on the droop. From that night on he was much more lenient in his judgment of the graybeards.

The long day always ended where it had begun...in the church. As in the dark of the morning, so now in the darkening night, John stood in his choir stall at the back of the church and said his appointed prayers, while up toward the front the white-robed religious chanted the Compline hour. Then came John Green Hanning's biggest moment, for the lay brothers filed toward the high altar and as the office of the day ended the cantor, in a rich, ringing voice, intoned the far-famed Cistercian "Salve," and as some seventy men took up the chant, the clear silvery velvet of the newest postulant's voice was heard in sacred song. Many an old monk softened his tones to listen, and many an aged brother straightened up as John Green Hanning put his heart on his tongue and sang to God's Mother with all that world of rapture and revelation that is held in the liquid silver of a true man's tenor voice.

John loved the moment, as carried away by the magic of the movement of this sublime prayer, he poured forth his love in the rich, rare velvet of his mellow voice.

"And so to bed." It had been a long day, a very long day. Eighteen hours makes a long day in any man's arithmetic. So John went to bed tired and John slept deeply, dreamlessly, refreshingly.

This sort of a day was all that John knew for about six weeks. Then the abbot called him and asked him what he thought of the Trappists and the Trappist's life. John, who was always most frank, said, "Not so bad," and the abbot surprised him with the speedy reply, "And that is just what the Trappists think of you. Not so bad. So tomorrow you may take the habit and from now on you will be known as Brother Mary Joachim."

On July 26, then, John Green Hanning put off his secular clothes and put on the brown.... I had almost said brown wool, but I glanced again at the date! Kentucky is warm in July, very warm. In fact, Kentucky is red hot. So Trappist lay brothers do not wear the Trappist brown wool; they wear a light robe of drill cotton and find that mighty heavy. So on July 26, John Green Hanning put off his secular clothes and put on the brown drill cotton of the Gethsemani Trappist lay brother, and on that day he lost his musical, melodious, tuneful name of John Green Hanning and took that of Joachim.

It has taken me a long time to get to that name. I have had to travel south and west and northeast again. I have had to wade through adolescence, early manhood, and middle age. I have had to call our hero John, John Green and John Green Hanning, "the Kentuckian," "the Quick One" and "Kentucky Jack," while all the time I have been itching to call him by the only name by which he will ever live, the only name under which he really lived, the name he took with him to the grave and under which he went to heaven. Now I can use it. Now I will use it. From now on he will be known either as Brother Mary Joachim, Brother Joachim, or simply, Joachim.

A Member of the Lost Battalion

On July 27, 1885, Brother Mary Joachim thought himself greatly changed. He had reason to think so, for his name was changed, his clothes were changed, his house was changed, all his habits of living were changed, even his facial appearance had changed, for now he wore a beard. But despite all these changes, Brother Mary Joachim had not changed. It is an easy matter to put off your coat, not quite so easy to put off your character. One can change his name in a minute, but not his nature. Brother Joachim had left much behind when he came to Gethsemani's cloister; he had left very much behind; but he had not left himself behind and very soon both he and the community would know it. A monk is not made in a month nor in a year; sometimes not even in a month of years, for like all solid and substantial things, true spirituality is a very slow and gradual growth.

Brother Joachim had changed his externals, and now that he had grown accustomed to the changes and had mastered the accidentals of the Trappist life, he could and did give more attention to the monks. They fascinated him, these living deadmen who had buried themselves alive in Gethsemani's Abbey.

A Trappist community is always an absorbing study, but to no one is it more intriguing than to him who contemplates living out the remainder of his days in their midst. It is a group of men one gets to know very intimately, and it is a group one never gets to know. You may live shoulder to shoulder with them for two score of years, and you know very little more at the end of the decades than you learned in the first few months. Where they come from, why they came, what motives now prompt their actions, are things that you may never know. Their mental modes and their emotional lives, their secret aims and ambitions, their aspirations and their desperations, their hearts and minds and wills, their triumphs and failures, their disappointments and disillusionments, their real reactions to men and manners...all these intimate and personal things that make an individual an individual are never known and never can be known; for the silence of the Trappist life is as deep as the sea and as full of mystery.

Yet you do come to know them quite intimately. Without any attempt at psychoanalysis, and always avoiding rash judgments, you cannot fail to catch the general character of each. The human face is ever eloquent. Its eyes that are filled with lights and shadows, its lips that express myriad moods, its subtle reflections of thoughts and emotions that pass and repass over the countenance in changes more varied than even cloud shadows on tree-covered hills—all contribute to make the human face revealing, and the tale it tells is always the story of the soul. Even the Stoics could not fail to express the petrifaction of their souls in the stolidity of their faces. So a Trappist, despite his sacred silence, is always speaking. Actions do speak louder than words, and so the general traits of each Trappist character is known to his fellow monks.

Almost a quarter of a century before Woodrow Wilson dreamed his "Fourteen Points," Brother Joachim found a "league of nations" at Gethsemani. And the wonder of it was that this league worked! It was a fusion of many nations working in perfect harmony for the greater glory of God and the good of the whole world. There were French, Germans, Italians, Irish, Swiss, Polish, Spanish, Mexicans, English, Lithuanians, and Americans—but all spoke the same tongue, the only Esperanto that has been universally used, the Trappist sign language.

In his many wanderings the ex-cowboy had met a multitude of men and had acquired the knack of classifying them rapidly. Here at Gethsemani he found subjects for his every class and some that called for the invention of new categories, for if a Trappist community is anything it is a conglomeration of many varied types. Here he found the doer and the dreamer, the poet and the peasant, the artist and the artisan. Here was the meditative Hamlet and the comrade more inclined to play the king's jester.

Brother Joachim saw them all. There were some whom he thought should never have seen the cloister for they had leadership written all over them—their walk, their carriage, the turn of their head. These he thought would have been captains of industry, commanders of men, or apostles whose mere presence would radiate energy and generate enthusiasm for the faith. A few others he knew were made for the cloister, or rather, the cloister was made for them, for they were timid souls, good souls, pure souls, but shy souls; and he knew that their meek demeanor would have had the heartless world running rough-shod over them and grinding them beneath a heedless heel.

Our hero was intrigued by these contrasts and contradictions. Here was a group of men united as no group out in the world could be, and yet alive with diversification. Despite their seeming drabness, Joachim soon saw that they were full of color and that, while their unity was astounding, so, too, was their variety. He found the pious and the practical doing the very same thing in their very different ways. Some he saw could model for holy pictures and for plaster-of-Paris saints, with heads bowed, hands folded and eyes cast down. These were usually the least practical and by no means necessarily the most pious. The others were animated refutations of the oft-repeated slur, "lazy monks." These were human dynamos, perpetual motion machines. It may have been that they were suffering from hyperactive thyroids, but more likely they had caught the voluminous truth contained in that sentence of two words—"Love serves!"

At any rate, Brother Joachim, being human, found the community at Gethsemani a most absorbing study. If there is one thing outstanding about these men who have consecrated themselves to the pursuit of the divine, it is their entire humanness. It is true that at first, because of their lackluster countenances, one or another made him regard them as the true mystics of the monastery. However, as time went on and the brother grew in wisdom and knowledge, he perceived that such good souls are more nearly morticians than monks. They wear smoked glasses and never see the grandeur and the glory in God's wondrous world, both animate and inanimate. They have never caught the full spirit of Jesus Christ, that *joie de vivre* that sends man and maid smashing through life with always a smile. Battle it is and battle it will ever be, but they know they are to be victorious for they are fighting with the Victor, Christ.

The community was a revelation and an inspiration to Joachim. He saw old men, some in brown and some in white, men whom time's hand had scarred, graying their beards and bending their shoulders, but men whose eyes shone with a splendor that enthusiastic youth can only envy and strive to emulate. For their souls were shining through these open windows, and the flame that was seen burning there made one bow in reverence. These were old men, old in years, old in the life, old in the love of God. These were the men, lay brothers and choir monks, who had become lost in God. These were the backbone and the very soul of the community. There were the true leaders of that "barricaded army that is following a star." These were the leaders of that justly styled "Lost Battalion"—a battalion lost to the world, lost to themselves, lost to life because they were lost in God. Brother Joachim felt not only a reverence and respect for these stiff-jointed and stooped old warriors, but in their presence he felt a holy and humble awe.

The middle group was that of men in their prime, men who were full of life and energy, but men who were ever denying themselves. To this class Joachim thought he should belong, for those in it were all workers and men of about his own age. The other class was the very young, and some of these were very, very young, mere boys who had come in their "teens" to begin the romance of all romances, that of daily falling deeper and deeper in love ...with God.

Yes, Brother Joachim grew to love these silent men of the monastery. Not all alike, of course, for all were not equally lovable. Some were reserved, distant and a trifle cold; these may be admired and loved with a Christian love, but they will never be really liked and often loved with the fullness of Christlike love. It takes all kinds of people to make up a world, and a Trappist monastery being a little world in itself must have all kinds of men.

To push on with Brother Joachim's formation then, we must tell how, after these months of assimilation, there came the day of self-expression. Brother had come to the realization that the men of the monastery were men and not creatures from another world. This may have decreased some of his awe and his ill-founded adoration, but it greatly increased his affection for the vast majority. I say the vast majority, for in any group there will always be one or two who grate on the nerves. A monastery may be the gate of heaven, but it is only the gate; and the monks are not angels...at least, not yet. Hence, while there may never be a fire there will often be heat, for it is the property of friction to generate heat, and what we so politely call "incompatibility" is actually friction.

One day Brother Joachim was sent to work with a little group in a field about a quarter of a mile from the monastery. A choir religious was the presiding officer. Joachim found nothing of appeal in this particular religious, and furthermore, our brother was tired. Have you ever noticed how offensive an inoffensive person can become when you are tired? And have you ever noticed that when people accidentally tread on your toes, they always manage to strike the most sensitive corn? Finally, have you ever noticed that when you are weary, really weary, people will always ask you to do the most difficult and the most wearying task? Well, Brother Joachim noticed all these things this particular afternoon and Brother Joachim's blood began to boil. The inoffensive and unoffending religious became very offensive and even offending to Joachim. His simple sign, which only meant "work here," said a whole world of things to our brother. Our brother bent to the task assigned, but southern eyes were blazing, for southern fires were lit.

As the moments went by, Joachim's temperature mounted. Anyone who knew him and his volcanic nature could see that while he had not yet erupted, smoke was gradually rolling up. As he worked he was reviewing the whole situation, and all the bile in his system was sending up poisonous vapors that in his eyes turned the world into a sickening yellowish green. Just when things seemed to have reached their lowest depths and Joachim had convinced himself that he had been wronged, insulted, even outraged, just when his whole being was one sensitive sore, the inoffensive and unoffending religious again, figuratively, stepped on our brother's very touchy toes, and, of course, pressed the corn! Instead of yellowish green, Joachim now saw red. Without a word to anyone, without a single sign, he strode from the place of work, stamped his angry way across the fields and the meadows and marched on and up to the house.

With each fierce stride the imagined injury grew. Before he had topped the hill on which the monastery sits, the wrong had assumed such proportions that Joachim determined it must be righted. While Joachim, it is true, was young in the community, yet this young monk must be shown that he was no baby. Southern fires were flaming; Joachim was once more John Green Hanning, the man who always "got even." Rushing to the tool house he seized a savage-looking hayfork, and with blazing eyes and firm, set jaw stalked to the front gate and there took up his stand. Through this gate the religious would have to pass on their way home from work. Joachim was going to "get even"; he was going to show this upstart monk how men from the South answer insult and injury.

There at the gate he stood, a formidable figure indeed, with his medieval monastic garb, his fiercely flashing eyes, his rigidly set mouth, and his hands firmly gripping a long, sharp, and very dangerous-looking hayfork. "He will not pass" was written all over him. The "Spirit of '76" and the "Minutemen of Lexington and Concord" could excellently have been modeled from him, as he fumed and fretted in angry impatience, awaiting the return of the monks.

The minutes passed, but no monks came. Joachim's tenseness grew. Fifteen minutes passed, and still no monks. Time was only feeding the fires that were already too fierce, and Joachim had started to pace the purposeless pace of a caged and angry lion...back and forth, back and forth, back and forth. When twenty minutes had passed, our brother was brought to a sudden halt by the appearance of the monastery's porter.

His appearance was surprising to Joachim but his sign was even more so. It told our stamping sentinel that the abbot wanted to see him and to see him right away. Joachim's jaw dropped. So, too, did the hayfork. After the first moment of surprise, our brother recovered his angry self and headed for the abbot's room with everything about him saying, "I'll tell the abbot a thing or two, also!"

Maybe he would have done so, if the abbot had been anyone but Dom Benedict Berger, the ironhanded molder of men. Much of the fire in the flaming Southerner was instantly smothered as the abbot fixed him with a piercing, searching, studying and very steady glance. After a moment he coldly asked Joachim what he was doing at the monastery gate. Our brother started to tell his story, but never finished it. Dom Benedict was too old a monk to need long explanations. He saw to the bottom of the trouble immediately, and he knew that it was in Joachim's heart. So he did the talking.

He told our brother much that afternoon, very much, even though Joachim as yet caught only the main outlines. He left the abbot's room that day fully alive to the realization that he had joined an army. He was now a member of the "Lost Battalion," a battalion lost to the world and the ways of the world, lost to self and all self-interests, lost to anything like temper or temperament, lost to life and love, lost to all—save God. Joachim realized that much; he could not help himself, for the abbot had been most insistent. Strong, stinging phrases had come out of the tense mouth of the old abbot and flashed before the mind of the amazed lay brother. There had been vehemence in the voice that said to him: "Don't learn the rule, live it!" "Obey!" "Be humble." "You are here to be a soldier of Christ; you are here to live your Confirmation." "Your own will has gone." "The only One you can't 'get even' with in this monastery is God!" There had been more, but only as paraphrase or amplification. At last Dom Benedict had said, "Do you understand?" and Joachim snapped, "I do."

But if the good abbot had had something like X-ray eyes and could have read the mind of his lay brother novice, he would have been surprised to read just what Joachim had understood. As he left the abbot's room and went to get the hayfork he had so unceremoniously dropped, Joachim was mad, very mad. Not with the choir religious—he was forgotten. Not with the abbot, who had just spoken to him as no man had ever spoken to him. He was raging mad with himself, and all because he had ever gotten mad. Joachim had caught the trend of the abbot's talk and it came to this: that he, Joachim, was rotten with pride and that this violent temper of his was nothing but pride's parade. That made him furious, for it was most true. But there was something more that Joachim understood and it was this: he was in an army, a member of the Lost Battalion; but, if the battalion was lost, it was not because it lacked a leader. Our brother understood most clearly that Dom Benedict Berger was a gray-haired, grizzled veteran, with a whiplash tongue, who wanted perfect obedience and profound humility.

What perfect obedience and profound humility were, Joachim did not know, but he had been made to realize that his leaving the place of work, stamping across the fields, seizing a hayfork and taking up his post at the gate with the determination to "get even" was neither obedience nor humility. He had been further made to realize that southern fires had to be much more carefully watched and much more controlled.

It was a somewhat chastened but not cowed Joachim who put the hayfork back in the tool shed. He had too much genuine manhood in him to be cowed. The verbal chastisement had made our brother mad; he was smarting all over. And in characteristic fashion he resolved a fierce resolve to "get even." This time it was with the abbot. Joachim determined "to show this Dom Benedict Berger that an American can be a good monk and that a fiery Kentuckian can be self-controlled." It was the beginning of Joachim's *metanoia*, his true conversion—the beginning of his purgation and thorough transformation.

It was not very much as yet, only a resolve; but it was a beginning. Years would pass before the *metanoia* was complete, and the good abbot who had fired Joachim to this fierce resolve would have long since received his reward. But the day would come when Joachim had proved to the hilt that an American cowboy can be a real contemplative, and a fiery Southerner a sterling Trappist.

The next morning when Joachim awoke, he thought himself a completely changed man. He thought that the determination taken yesterday afternoon marked the final end of his days of temper and tempestuousness. Poor Joachim! If he only knew! But he had made up his mind, and he wrongly believed that this resolution was his metamorphosis. He had yet to learn that between resolution and realization there yawns an unbridgeable gorge, and that down into that deep valley, which is death to self, he would have to go. Poor Joachim! He still had much to learn, very much; for let it be remembered that while he was a man of thirty-six years, he was only a babe of three or four months in the world where all must become as little children, but where this childhood is sometimes never attained until ripe old age.

Before Joachim had realized his resolution he would groan much. In fact, on this very first day of the resolution he gave vent to many a groan. But these groanings were not so much the evidence of a death struggle as they were of the pangs of birth; for vindictiveness was slowly, very slowly, bringing forth a saint.

Metanoia—
The Molding of a Man

At first I was going to title this chapter "Metamorphosis." But, like Shakespeare, I do not care to repeat. We already have had the metamorphosis. It took place on July 26. For metamorphosis is a change of form, and when John Green Hanning had his head shaved and grew a beard, when he had his secular clothes taken off him and the Trappist brown drill put upon him, when he lost his nice name of John Green Hanning and received that of Brother Mary Joachim, we had a complete change of form. But before Brother Mary Joachim becomes the saintly Mary Joachim, we must have more than a mere change of form. We must have a complete revolution of mental modes, a revaluation of all life's values, a thorough transmutation of feelings, intentions and opinions, and an absolute reversal and reformation of aims, ambitions, and aspirations. We must have a total transformation of the soul...and the only word for that is the Greek word transliterated...*metanoia*.

Christ's first call was for a *metanoia*, and throughout his public preachings *metanoia* was frequently heard. The English versions translate the word as "repent" or "do penance," but neither of these convey Christ's full message, nor translate his real thought. He did not call for mere suffering and sorrow; he did not want mere bodily pain. What he wanted and what he still wants is that men "be converted and live." Conversion is a *metanoia*...a change of heart, mind and will. When Christ said, "Unless you do penance, you shall all likewise perish," he was not talking about the necessity of bodily macerations, but about the universal necessity for *metanoia*...a complete transformation of soul.

If penance consists in bodily castigations, then the Flagellantes of New Mexico are better penitents than the Trappists of Kentucky, for the Flagellantes scourge their body to blood while the Trappist only bleeds his heart.

The Trappist wears no hair shirt nor girdle of pointed steel; his whip of little cords he very rarely employs, for instruments of torture are practically unknown to him. He never does the dramatic, or rather the melodramatic, thing of fashioning himself a cross and fastening himself thereto; but he must crucify his spirit, spiking his soul to the very real cross of perpetual self-denial. He must flay his heart to rawness, ripping out many of the licit loves of the years, and scourging away all the clinging affections for the world and the things of the world. He must smash the scales of his mind, those lying scales that time has given him, which weigh all worth by the weights of material accomplishments and proud personal achievement. He must shatter his sense of values, that deceiving and deceptive sense which puts a price of dollars and cents on all things tangible and is ever looking for profit and gain. He must tear off of his being those grasping tentacles of acquisitiveness that are ever stretching out in their greed to have and to hold. When he has stripped himself naked of self, then he can stand ready to be clothed with Christ. That is the Trappist's penance.

A Trappist has his external penances, many of them. He has his plain diet, his bed of boards with its mattress of straw, his manual labor and his perpetual silence, his fastings and his watchings...but these without *metanoia* would be practices of penance and not penance itself; and in this case, practice would never make perfect! These without *metanoia* would be semblances of piety without piety's substance, for they would not be the self-denial that leads to sanctity; rather they would be the sinful and selfish self-expression and self-indulgence which we know as sadism.

The prime purpose of much of the Trappist's penance is to aid his contemplation. For if a man would be a great mystic, he must first become a great ascetic; he must die to self, and dying to self is but another name for *metanoia*. Self—that assertive, sin-inclined self, which was generated in Eden when Adam pleased a woman but angered God—never dies. It cannot be killed, but if one is to be a true contemplative, it must be kept in a state of general coma. To keep that self in coma and to maintain his *metanoia*, his complete transformation of soul, a Trappist fasts, watches and keeps silence.

It is true that a Trappist has another and a higher purpose in his penances, but this can only come later. Before one can lay down his life for the beloved, he must first fall in love. That is why a Trappist first lights the sacrificial fires in his own heart by contemplation, before he lays himself on the altar of suffering for a total consummation. Before he becomes a vicarious victim who slays himself that a sinning world might be "converted and live," he must first see that world through the eyes of God, have mercy on it with the mercy of God, and love it with that burning love that flames in the heart of God. But before any human can become so divine, he must effect a true *metanoia*.

Metanoia is the gateway to real life. Passing through it, one acquires new standards—the standards of God. The mind is made hungry for truth, but for the truths of eternity. The will is made greedy for beauty, but for true beauty, the *splendor veritatis*, that can be had and held only in the brightness of the beatific vision, in the light of him who said, "I am truth." The memory is made rich with treasure, for it is stored with golden scenes from the life of Christ. Thus is the whole man changed, and to keep that change permanent the wise man cloisters himself. Not to lock himself in, but to lock the world out. He has found "the treasure in a field," so he "goes, sells all that he has, and buys that field." To effect this *metanoia* in the soul of Brother Mary Joachim, Dom Benedict Berger gave his attention in 1885 and 1886.

He effected it. But there were days, many of them, when the good abbot feared paranoia for himself rather than the expected *metanoia* for Brother Joachim. For our novice had many ideas of his own, and the most difficult thing in the world is to convince an uncontrolled man that he needs control.

Brother Joachim was hardly ready as yet to be acquainted with the secondary end of Trappist austerities. For before one can become a sacrificial lamb, one must first be a lamb, and there was much about Joachim that was neither meek nor mild. The abbot was going to teach him asceticism before he tried to teach him mysticism, and in this he was wise. We do teach people arithmetic before we introduce them to calculus, do we not? One must first know decimals before he can use logarithms. So, too, in the spiritual life; if one would be reborn, he must first die; and to bring about this death, Dom Benedict planned his course.

No doubt, not everyone will approve the abbot's methods. But let it be remembered that a wrongly-knitted bone cannot be reset unless it is rebroken. Some call such an operation a gamble; for nature can prove very stubborn at times and seems to resent the interference of man. And if such be the case with the body, it is doubly true of the soul. Hence, only the most skillful of soul surgeons, only those most intimate with God should ever dare the rebreaking and the resetting of a soul. Dom Benedict took the dare and went about his work with all the surety of a master.

One day our novice was working in the kitchen where the meals for seculars are prepared, and he was working very diligently with a large set of rather fragile dishes. Joachim was never what you would call strong, but he was always energetic and on this particular day his energy far exceeded his strength. He piled dish on dish on dish, and then started to carry the towering tray to the shelves where the dishes were stored. There was a crash, as tray and tower fell from wet fingers and went flying in many pieces over the kitchen floor. Joachim picked up the pieces and, observing the rule of the house, took what he had ruined to the Reverend Abbot.

Dom Benedict was an opportunist. He had been waiting for something just like this. He looked at the fragments dispassionately, then at the brother still more dispassionately, and then most dispassionately said, "That is too bad, Brother. No doubt it was an accident. But we do not carry accident insurance. You may write to your folks and beg from them the price to cover the damages."

Joachim was aghast. He glared at the abbot. There was a flash in southern eyes, but there was silence. Quickly he got off his knees, quickly he bowed to the abbot, and very quickly he left the room. He was seething. He flew down the corridor. A dozen or more thoughts chased one another through Joachim's mind—burning, biting thoughts; quick, stabbing, flashes of thoughts that had him shaking with rage. "He! Joachim! Thirty-six years of age! Beg from his father! He beg! For some dishes! Beg from home! Tell them that he had broken some plates! Ask them for money! What was the abbot trying to do anyhow? Is this what they call religion? What would the folks think?"

If Dom Benedict Berger had paged through the records of all the monks and all the monasteries from the days of Anthony, Benedict, and

Francis down to de Rance and La Trappe, he would never have found a penance better calculated to make or break Brother Mary Joachim than: "Beg from your folks the money to cover the damages." How those words seared themselves into Joachim's soul. They would have broken that soul, broken it beyond resetting, were it not for the fact that Joachim was vindictive—the man who always "got even."

For hours and hours Joachim squirmed. He wanted to be humble, he told himself, but he was not going to become a worm. He was ready to make reparation, even though reparation was not strictly due, since the whole thing was an accident. He would willingly perform any public penance before the entire community; but why should he wash his linen before the whole world? Why parade and placard the pious practices of a monastery for an unbelieving and scoffing countryside? He, the man who went away to be a hero, would be the laughingstock of the parish. What was the abbot thinking of anyhow?

Suddenly Joachim stopped and exclaimed, "So that is it, is it? He thinks I haven't the courage. Well, I'll show him!" Then he hurriedly seized pen and paper, and begged.

It did break his soul, broke it wide open. This act of humility, performed in the vicious pride of vindictiveness, had many effects on many people, but the greatest was on Brother

Mary Joachim himself. It was the real beginning of his *metanoia*—the molding of a man of God. As the years mounted, many memories faded from the storehouse of Brother Joachim's mind, but there was one thing that he never forgot and that was that he was made to beg.

The abbot most likely sent back the money with a note that was a series of chuckles rather than a page of sentences, and both fathers of this grown boy, the natural and the spiritual, enjoyed a hearty laugh at their boy's expense. But expense it was! No one but Joachim and God know what a mighty expense it was. But it was money well spent as the after years proved.

According to physics, before electricity will flow, the negative pole of one battery must be joined to the positive pole of another. In fact, to have a battery at all, there must be an anode and a cathode. So, too, in magnets and magnetism, the positive and negative come into play. As in physics, so also in life and very especially in the spiritual life, the positive and negative must be balanced and conjoined before we can have anything like dynamic energies or magnetic souls.

To electrify a person with spiritual energies, the anode and the cathode must both be present. Spiritually dynamic men are produced only when the positive and negative terminals of suffering and joy, dark trial and laughing triumph, failure and success, are so conjoined that the soul is always fluid. God works this in nature and likewise in the supernature. With too much sunshine the rose withers; with too much rain it wilts. So, too, with the soul. It must have contraction, for it is proud; it must have expansion, for it loves. It needs desolations, for it is grasping, greedy, and miserly; it needs consolations, for it is not yet divine. And God gives both. Nature must have balance, its sunshine and its rain; so, too, supernature.

These are the truths that a spiritual father must always have in mind. He must remember that in the soul of every person there sleeps a sinner and a saint. It is his work to paralyze the sinner and energize the saint. But he will never do either if he does not connect the negative pole of chastisement with the positive pole of encouragement. If he will use the rod, he must also reward. To mold a man into a man of God a curb is needed—a bitter, sharp and biting curb—but so, too, is the spur. Dom Benedict was a wise spiritual father. He had shown Joachim the actuality that existed in his soul; he now threw light on the possibilities that slumbered there, as he congratulated him on his heroic act of humility and endeavored to channel the strong tides of determination that swept the soul of this novice lay brother and set them flowing toward God.

The abbot was experienced. He knew that a sense of duty would produce a soldier, but it would never produce a saint; for duty done is service, but sanctity is love. The abbot had no need of soldiers, so he set himself to that ever difficult task of blowing to flame the tiny spark of love for God that slumbers in the soul of everyone. The difficulty arises from the fact that God is so intimate that he is unknown. People do not know God. God is within them and without them. God is all around them. People are steeped in and saturated with God. In very truth, in God each person "lives and moves and has his being," and yet does not know him. The omnipresent God is absent to most, the personal God is most impersonal, and the most loving of fathers lives unloved, because the individual never seems to grasp the truth that God is *his* God.

For a whole lifetime some people use words that represent no objective reality to them. They pray more by instinct than intelligence, so their prayer is perfunctory and cold. God is dim and distant, a dweller in a world apart, a being who lives in some remote realm beyond those distant stars and those measureless skies. They forget that God became a baby, that he wrapped his infinity in flesh that we might learn the secret of life and love. These men never seem to realize that God became incarnate that we might incarnate our ideas of God. But until they do incarnate their ideas of God and make him personal to themselves, they will always remain mediocre men and frigid worshipers.

To really love calls for red blood, and only a passionate, personal love for Jesus Christ will make one a saint. Love is the body, the soul, the whole substance of sanctity. The infatuate and the affectionate might live for God, but the lover is glad to die for him. Sanctity demands passion, real daring and fire. But how kindle that fire? How elevate selfish and calculating man to the frenzy of reckless daring? How arouse man to the mad passion of a raging love? Those are the riddles that worry the director of souls. Those are some of the riddles that gave Dom Benedict pause, as he bent to the task of making Brother Mary Joachim realize that God, the Almighty, had an infinite, eternal, personal, passionate, absorbing love for Brother Mary Joachim.

Dom Benedict knew that unless he made the all-living God live for Joachim, he might have a man who would live in the monastery, work on the monastery farm, attend all the monastery exercises, answer all the monastery bells and make every bow that the monastery regulations prescribe, but he would not have a Trappist monk. Years in the service had shown the abbot that until the All-reality, who is God, loses his tremendous unreality in the mind of an individual, pious practices are religiously performed but no true sanctity is ever produced.

He saw passion, daring, and fire in the soul of this Southerner, and he knew that if he could once make the personal God really personal to Joachim, America would have a real American saint. But how to do it? How make the statement "God loves you" lose its triteness and pulse with its staggering truth? How make Joachim realize that Jesus Christ lived and died—yes, all for Joachim? That the infinite God was absorbed in Joachim's watchings and walkings, his goings out and his comings in? That the King of all creation was a suppliant for Joachim's warm affection and virile love?

Joachim had heard all these things before, but for him, as for most of us, they had remained statements of truths, heard but never assimilated. They had struck the tympanum of the ear, been registered in the brain and stored in the memory, but had never gotten into the blood or gone down deep into the soul. They remained static statements and had never become dynamic facts.

Dom Benedict knew that if he could make what had taken on the palsy of the prosaic pulse with a personal appeal, Joachim would cease being almost good and begin to become really great. So he started, started slowly. He gave Joachim a riddle rather than a revelation.

He equivalently told our brother that he must come to realize that the Trappist life was not something but Someone; and with the wisdom of the truly wise, having dropped his seed, the abbot waited for it to germinate. It would be years before Joachim fully understood that statement, but the abbot was satisfied. He knew that the oak which is cradled in the heart of the acorn becomes a giant only after years.

The abbot was sparing of words. He gave Joachim an idea; that was all, no elaboration, no explanation, no amplification. But he knew that if Joachim ever assimilated that idea it would burst into an ideal, and this, in turn, would become an agony and a luxury as it tore his soul with the raptures and the tortures of love. When Joachim had come to the realization that the Trappist life is not penitence but the passionate abandon of love, when he had come to the point where his every step fitted perfectly into the footprints of the Man who walked Judean hills, when Joachim's every breath was for, in and through Jesus Christ, then Joachim would be the Trappist that Dom Benedict wanted and planned for, as he said, "Life at Gethsemani is not something, it is Someone."

But the good abbot would not leave Joachim with only a puzzle. That would have been poor pedagogy and rather cruel. He gave the novice brother two practices, and these were the practices that ultimately solved the riddle and turned the real puzzle into a revelation. He gave Joachim the Rosary and the Way of the Cross. These two were the positive poles that he connected with the negative ones of mortification and humiliation. The negative paralyzed the sinner, the positive energized the saint, and the conjunction of both proved Joachim's perfect *metanoia*.

The Deepening of a Heart

It may seem strange to some that an abbot of a contemplative order should give a brother aspiring to become a contemplative such commonplace practices as the Rosary and the Way of the Cross. Every Catholic has said the Rosary and has made the Way of the Cross. Some will never allow a sun to set before they have performed both of these practices, and yet they do not consider themselves contemplatives, and would never think of becoming Trappists. How explain, then, this action of Dom Benedict Berger? He gave commonplace practices of piety to a man aspiring to become a contemplative. Was he wrong?

No, indeed, he was not wrong. We are wrong; for the moment we hear "contemplation," we immediately think of John of the Cross, Teresa of Avila, and Francis de Sales, forgetting that there is contemplation and contemplation. We have come to associate the word with the higher form of mystical prayer, thinking only of those gifts of God which cannot be acquired no matter how long nor how earnestly one strives, and forgetting all about that which is within the range of everyone. A Trappist is a man, and only a man, hence, he aspires to active contemplation, not passive. Active contemplation is within the compass of man; passive depends entirely upon the liberality of God. Visions, ecstasies and raptures, revelations and stigmatizations are not the object of a Trappist's strivings; but close, intimate, heart-to-heart union with God is. A Trappist looks not for the extraordinary gifts of God; he looks only for God. He sees him not in the light of vision, but through such commonplace practices as the Rosary well said and the Way of the Cross well made. To make a contemplative—an active contemplative—out of an ex-cowboy, Dom Benedict chose the most efficacious means possible, the Rosary and the Way of the Cross.

The abbot did not want an ecstatic, he wanted a man of prayer, and the only way a man of prayer is made is by praying. Rapt in ecstasy, Joachim would have been of little practical value around a farm. If all the Trappist lay brothers became visionaries, they might fail to see the cows and the sheep, the mules and the swine, the rows of corn that must be cultivated and the countless vines that must be sprayed. A Trappist community, you know, is self-supporting; and if all became mystics, in the common acceptance of the term, I greatly fear that the community would soon collapse. There is hardly any doubt that passive contemplation in a farmer spells ruin for the farm, for how can a man plow a field, and plow it well, while lifted out of himself and raised to the third heaven? Mules often refuse to obey a man; what would they do to a mystic? No, passive contemplation is not the end and the aim of a Trappist lay brother; active contemplation is. And Joachim was set toward that goal by an experienced guide who gave him the Rosary and the Way of the Cross.

Dom Benedict knew the Trappist life and Dom Benedict knew the human heart, and so he gave ordinary practices to make a man extraordinary. He knew that man's greatest sin is one of omission and not of commission. He knew that men humbly confess their many exterior faults and failures, that they sorrowfully and sincerely accuse themselves of violating this precept and that command; but he also knew that men seldom accuse themselves of the sin that hurts the heart of God the most and the one that men most frequently commit...the sin of "not loving." He was going to get Joachim to avoid that sin, so he gave him the two people to love—Jesus, the God-man, and Mary, his Mother.

The abbot followed the wise method of

indirection and suggestion. He did not want sentimentality; he did not want pietism; he did not want mechanical recitation. So he set Joachim thumbing his beads and making the stations, knowing that, if this firebrand from the South would be faithful to these two practices and be thoughtful while he practiced them, he would one day be a man of prayer, an active contemplative, a real Trappist. He would be a passionate lover of Jesus Christ and his Mother, Mary. Both were too manly for anything but real religion, so Dom Benedict gave Joachim God through his senses, his mind and his will.

The abbot saw that Joachim had a big heart, but the abbot also saw that it would have to be deepened, dredged, and drained before it could love God the way a Trappist brother should love God. He knew that he had already broken it once when he made him beg; he also knew that he would have to break it again and again before that heart would be empty of Joachim and filled with Jesus Christ. Here was a man of high spirits, very high spirits; mules, monks and masters knew that. But what these forgot, Dom Benedict remembered—namely, that high spirits make high sanctities. That is why even though some in the community resented Joachim with his temper and his tempestuousness, the abbot rejoiced to see these fires and their flashes, for, if he could control these, he would have a lay brother who really loved his God and not a man living in a lay brother's garb.

Joachim was stubborn; Dom Benedict liked that, for stubbornness can be converted into a virtue and become real strength. Joachim was violent; Dom Benedict considered this an asset, for violence can easily be turned into zeal. Joachim was filled with self-assurance; Dom Benedict knew that this was a great blessing for one who sets out to grasp God. The abbot looked upon Joachim as excellent material for an active contemplative, but material that needed much molding, so he gave it. Dom Benedict was determined to shape vindictiveness into virtue, turn that flaming temper into fixed determination, make of this raging fire a controlled furnace, and blow the flame in Joachim's heart to a fury.

The kitchen, wherein the meals for seculars are prepared, loomed as something of a nemesis for our good brother. Here he had broken some dishes and thus led to the first breaking of his heart. Here he had another mishap. One day he was told to give some old scraps of meat a slow bake. Joachim obeyed, very literally; he baked them for three or four days! But exact obedience did not prompt this, a treacherous memory did. Joachim had forgotten all about the meat, for the oven, even in what is called "the secular kitchen" of a Trappist monastery, is very seldom used. However, this meat turned out to be something that Joachim never forgot. Once again he had to go to the abbot with what he had ruined. It was a black, burned, dirty-looking mess that he displayed before the keen eyes of Dom Benedict. As he knelt before his abbot, holding a large pan of something that looked like greasy charcoal, Joachim was the picture of humility, or at least, of humiliation.

"What is it?" snapped the abbot.

"Meat," snapped back Joachim.

"It doesn't look like it," growled the abbot.

"I burned it," growled Joachim.

"Eat it," barked the abbot, and Joachim was silent. He looked up at the abbot, then down at the mess, then up at the abbot again. After a moment, he got up from his knees and as he was bowing to his abbot, he managed to squeeze out between tightly closed teeth, "Yes, Reverend Father." Then Joachim left the room.

Holding the pan in his two hands, Joachim stamped down the corridor to the accompaniment of: "Eat it." "Eat it." "Eat it." When he got to the kitchen, he threw the pan on the table and, picking up a bit of the charcoaled meat, he asked, "Eat this?" And then, as he was about to break into a rage, he stopped, slowly replaced the cinder of meat and musingly said to himself, "So that is it, is it?

THE DEEPENING OF A HEART

Thinks he will crush me, does he?" Then with his wonted energy he exclaimed, "Well, I'll show him!" And the vindictive Joachim made arrangements to have some of the black mess served to him every day in the refectory.

How he managed it, I do not know. Neither did he. He could only say that it took him six months to dispose of it, but dispose of it he did, right down to the last cinder. And what was the result? A deepening of the heart!

Let me explain. A resolve taken in the heat of resentment will not sustain a man for six months. That fierce determination vanished after the first few days of gritty charcoal, and then Joachim had to face the very practical question as to whether or not he was biting off his own nose to spite his own face. The black crusts were not sticking in the abbot's teeth; so all this vindictiveness was proving a boomerang unless—and here was the deepening process—unless Joachim found another motive for spoiling his every meal with cinders and ashes. Often during the six months he was compelled to ask himself, "Isn't this madness?" "Isn't it nonsense?" These were not mere rhetorical questions; they demanded answers. And after some thought Joachim gave the answers. Ultimately he was able to say, "No, this is not all nonsense. I am not really getting even with the abbot. I am obeying, and that is a virtue. I am obeying not a man, not the abbot, not Dom Benedict Berger, I am obeying God." With that, Joachim was able to take another bite of his gritty, never-to-be-forgotten slow bake.

Joachim was getting God-conscious. He was at the beginning of the process that would ultimately lead him to the solution of the riddle which the abbot had given him. Joachim was thinking more and more about Christ, and this would one day bring him to the realization that the Trappist life is truly not something, but Someone. These penances were medicinal in more than the strictly technical sense. They were making our brother think, and in conjunction with his Way of the Cross and the Rosary, they were deepening his mind and his heart. The more these penances purged away Joachim, the more they brought in Jesus and Mary, and the heart deepened.

Yet no one skyrockets to sanctity. And, though six months on a diet of charcoaled meat may seem long to some, Joachim did not soar to the heights he was one day to reach. The climb to sanctity has never been and never will be a perfectly straight ascent; for man is man, and, therefore, before he reaches the heights, he is going to fall, and to fall many a time. Joachim did. He fell often, and by his falling showed himself a man; but he picked himself up and started on again, and thus showed himself a monk. He knew that he was a spitfire, and while he could defend many of his outbreaks subjectively, he knew that objectively he should be more patient if he was to grow "in the likeness of Christ."

Here was the situation. Joachim was not a big man physically. He was not what you would call a strong man, but he was a neat, energetic and efficient worker. Yet he had to work with men, some of whom would never be neat, others who could do nothing energetically, and still others who could never be efficient. All of this irritated. Joachim did not become angry just for the sake of becoming angry. He had his reasons—many of them; and most of them were two-legged and brown-robed. There is never an effect without a cause, never an explosion without an ignition. A spark of some sort must strike dynamite before there is a blast; and the awkwardness of some, the slowness of others and the inefficiency of still others were the sparks that set off our package of dynamite from old Kentucky. He was impatient, very impatient; and he knew it. To find himself showing it daily made him all the more impatient, for he was conscious of his character defect and was striving to overcome it. Environment was working its effect.

One cannot stay out in the rain without getting wet, nor out in the sun without becoming tanned. Neither can one live long in a community of quiet, disciplined, patient men, without becoming conscious of one's own impatience, disquiet, and lack of discipline. But there was another presence that was affecting Joachim. He was often in the sacramental Presence and lived conscious of the omnipresence of God. This God-consciousness and the constant contact with men of God were making Joachim gentle, and though he slipped often, he rose just as often, and it was the getting up that really counted!

About 1888, Joachim was very happy, for he was making steady effort and thought that he was making steady progress. For weeks now he had not openly erupted. He was mentally patting himself on the back and metaphorically throwing out his chest over his victory, when the abbot sent for him. Dom Benedict had been visited with a stroke of apoplexy and was paralyzed except for his right arm. He called Joachim this day and asked our brother to shave him. Joachim gladly acquiesced and began to lather the abbot with a quiet mind, for he knew that he had not manifested any impatience for weeks.

Dom Benedict, however, wanted more than a shave this particular morning. He wanted to talk with Joachim and, crippled though he was, he wanted to do some pruning. He knew Brother Joachim better than Brother Joachim knew himself. He knew that Joachim was proud of his acquired patience, so he determined to prick the pretty bubble our brother had blown for himself and have it break before his very eyes.

"Brother," said the abbot, as Joachim stropped the razor preparatory for the first stroke, "you'll have to do better."

Joachim almost slashed the strop. He was startled. But he had gained some wisdom and some prudence, so he kept silent. Very quietly he came over to the abbot, placed his hand on the abbot's temple, and began to shave him.

"Yes," went on the abbot, "you'll have to do much better." Then with every stroke of the razor the abbot pointed out some fault to our poor brother, who thought he had made such marvelous progress. "You're proud. When will you learn humility? Every manifestation of your nasty temper is nothing but a manifestation of your nastier pride."

Joachim's jaw squared. Every sentence of the abbot's was a stab into his sensitive soul. Before he had half completed the shaving, his brain was racing and his heart was pounding. Inwardly he was starting to rebel. It was all so unjust, he thought. The abbot was not only unjust, he was unreasonable and untrue. He had not merited this. For months now he had reined in his temper with a merciless hand. No one had seen any sign of it for weeks. Still the abbot went on and on. His accusations were little more than glittering generalities, and Joachim soon recognized them as such. Any man can be called "proud," for every man is proud. "Learn humility" can be barked at any monk, for every son of Adam needs continual lessons in this virtue.

He finished the left side of the abbot's face and shifted his position to the abbot's right side. Had Dom Benedict been watching closely he would have seen by the very tenseness of Joachim's every move that he was seething, that he was holding himself in only by fierce will power. But Dom Benedict was not watching that closely, so he went on with his pruning and purgative process.

Joachim managed to stroke with a steady hand and had almost finished the shaving when the abbot, to emphasize a point, raised the only hand he could move and shook a warning finger under Joachim's very nose. Perhaps Joachim would have taken even this had not the abbot's shaking finger struck his firm-set chin. This flick of the finger was the spark that exploded our brother. Lightning that had its hilt in Joachim's heart and its point at the abbot's eyes flashed. Joachim lifted the razor, and shaking it before the abbot's startled face said in a passion-filled, deadly voice, "Put down that hand. Put down that hand." The abbot did. "If you move so much as an eyelash, I'll slash you from ear to ear," and a fear-filled abbot was looking into the face of the man who always "got even."

In this menacing attitude Joachim stood for a moment, then with a brush of the towel that was almost a blow, he wiped the tiny bit of remaining lather from the abbot's face and after slamming down the razor, stormed from the room.

As the door banged a very loud bang behind the retreating form of Joachim, Dom Benedict let out the breath he had been holding ever since he had heard the tense command, "Put down that hand" and had seen the cold steel of a keen-edged razor quivering before his face. He had seen Joachim in a fury often; he had never before seen him in the deadly, cold anger of a murderous madman.

For a full thirty minutes he was left alone. Then came a knock on his door—not a bold, demanding knock, but rather a subdued and timid knock. He gave the signal for the party to enter and was surprised to see none other than our Brother Mary Joachim. He came in, knelt down, and as he looked at his abbot, his eyes filled and he wept as he said, "Reverend Father, I am sorry and ashamed. My temper, my pride, my fiery blood got the better of me. I am truly sorry; forgive me and give me a penance."

Then Dom Benedict Berger smiled and said, "I forgive you, Brother; and for your penance, go to Holy Communion tomorrow morning."

The next morning Joachim received Holy Communion, and again told his God that he was ashamed of himself and very much puzzled by this abbot of his, who, for a penance, had given him so glorious a privilege. But Joachim was talking to the right person about the wrong person. Little did Joachim realize that all this puzzling procedure was due to God rather than to Dom Benedict. Little did Joachim realize what was happening to his heart as he fell into impatience and rose to repentance, as he was crushed by his abbot and consoled by Communion, made miserable by his own hotheadedness and still more miserable by his abbot's humiliations. Little did Joachim know that God was deepening, dredging, and draining his heart.

As he so frequently does, God was working through paradoxes. To make Joachim meek and mild, he was allowing him to be violent and vindictive. To humble him, he was allowing him to be proud. To bring him to the virtue of penitence, he was allowing him the vice of impatience. Joachim wept openly only once during these years, and that was after he had threatened his abbot with a razor, but interiorly he wept often. After every violent outburst, he was filled with chagrin and self-disgust, and this chagrin and self-disgust only angered him the more and made him a more ready victim for the next attack. Poor Joachim went through torture during these early years; but it made him realize that when he relied on his Samsonlike self he was leaning on a broken reed, and what he called strength of will was weakness. Yes, it was a cruel way, but it was a sure way.

In 1890, however, God used another method of attack. To dredge the heart of Joachim even deeper, God used death. On January 26, he called Joachim's father home. He died at Gethsemani as a "family brother," that is, one who lives at the Abbey, does what work he can around the monastery and, except for vows and the religious habit, is practically a member of the community. John Hanning, Sr., was buried at Gethsemani's Abbey, and his son had the pleasure and the pain of seeing his own father buried as one of his own brothers, with Trappists in white singing, and Trappists in brown praying, as the body was lowered into a Trappist grave.

As Joachim stood by the simple cross that marked his father's grave, he saw with the clarity of vision that "one thing alone is necessary." For there was nothing that made him more God-conscious than the mound of earth that hid his father's clay. Often he went there to pray and think—to think of life in the light of death—and it was this reviewing of his father's many years that gave greater meaning to Joachim's remaining days.

His father had lived a long life and a very interesting one. When but five years of age, he was brought to this country from Ireland by his two half brothers. As was the custom of the day, these two bound the five-year-old youngster to a tailor in New York City and betook themselves to that other Irish stronghold, Philadelphia. For eight years young John lived with this tailor, and, while growing in years and in strength, he grew also in the knowledge of the needle, the scissors and the cloth. When thirteen, he considered his apprenticeship over and made his way to Philadelphia to find his half brothers. He found them and for a short while all three lived together, but for some unknown reason, young John soon decided to shift for himself. His half brothers encouraged him in this decision and sent him off with their best wishes and ten dollars of their good money. John managed to keep their wishes, but before he had cleared the limits of this city of brotherly love, a sharper had relieved him of the money.

From reminiscences given during his lifetime, it was gathered that he drifted from town to town and city to city, always working as a tailor. Drifting south and west, he stayed some time in Cincinnati, Ohio, and in Louisville, Kentucky. From the latter city, he struck out for

Lebanon, Kentucky, where he opened a little tailor shop of his own.

He did well at Lebanon, very well indeed! He gained an education, some wealth, and a wife. The students of St. Mary's College patronized his shop and he, when he could, patronized St. Mary's College. These sporadic college courses, coupled with a voracious appetite for reading, rendered the young Irish immigrant well educated. While attending St. Mary's he met Mary Jane Hagan, the lovely daughter of a well-to-do farmer. This meeting culminated in marriage in 1840.

For the next seventeen years, John and Jane lived and prospered in Lebanon. Six of their nine children were born here, and from all appearances, one would have said that the Hanning couple would live and die in Lebanon. But John had too big a heart and too many acquaintances in and about Lebanon to suit Jane. He was the good-natured fellow who would "go on your paper" whenever you needed money. Many of those papers John Hanning had to pay off and, while Jane believed in Christian charity, she knew that it began at home. So in 1857, she persuaded John to go to Owensboro, buy some land there, and become a farmer. On the thousand acres of land that he purchased, he very successfully conducted a tobacco farm for twelve long years. But nothing succeeds like success, so John

Hanning built a distillery in 1869, and produced the famous John Hanning Whiskey, which brought him not only fame but also fortune.

In 1880, when he was seventy-five years old and had just taken on a $40,000 note for a fellow distiller (Mary Jane had changed John's habitat but hadn't changed his heart!), his distillery went up in flames. Despite his advanced age he might have rebuilt, but he had to pay off immediately the $40,000 note for which he had become liable. He paid it off, sold the name of his whiskey to a corporation, and retired from active business.

In 1882, his wife died. In 1885, John Green left him for the Trappist monks, and in 1886 his baby girl, Sarah Corina, married. In 1888, Mary Catherine, the only girl at home, became Mrs. Hough B. Campbell. Henry, the baby boy, was now twenty-seven, so John Hanning, Sr., felt free. In 1889, though over eighty-five years of age, he went to Our Lady of Gethsemani's Abbey to live as a "family brother" and to prepare for a holy death.

Death is a revealer, and while many claim that it shows them only the emptiness of life, to Joachim it showed life's fullness. Better than any spiritual book was this simple cross and this heaped-up earth; more eloquent than abbot, choir monk, or preacher of retreats was this silent mound. His father's grave kept saying to him, "Time is short! Spend it well!"

Despite this heavy loss, God dredged deeper. Eighteen ninety's winter melted into spring, spring blossomed into summer, and summer was about to mellow into autumn when death struck again. This time it took his spiritual father, and as Joachim dug Dom Benedict Berger's grave, he recalled every penance and every tongue lashing this stern molder of monks had given him. With each shovel of earth, Joachim looked deeper into his own heart and was surprised to see there the love that had grown, all unknown to himself, for this man who had flayed him with words and scourged him with penance, but had broken him of pride and introduced him to God.

Our brother was not dry-eyed as he saw the abbot's body lowered into the grave. This death was Joachim's full birth; for Dom Benedict, cold and silent in death, spoke to our lay brother with a warmth that he had never used before. "For God! For God! All for God!" seemed to flame from the marble lips of the dead abbot and set Joachim's pulses pounding. Every lesson that Dom Benedict had taught him, from the day of the hayfork incident to the day of the brandished razor, now lived for Joachim with a force that they had never had before. He knew that his training had amounted to almost a persecution, but as the cross was planted over the mound and the last spade pat given to the dank earth, Joachim realized that the soil covered his molder, his maker, and, under God, his savior.

Francis Thompson with a keenness given only to the mystic and the poet, saw a truth and sang in soothing rhythm:

> The falling acorn buds the tree,
> The falling rain, the greenery,
> The fern-plants moulder, where the ferns
>   arise;
> For nothing lives but something dies,
> And nothing dies but something lives,
> Till skies be fugitives.

Never were his last lines more true than when Dom Benedict died; for then Joachim, the saint, was fully born. Yes, the saintly Joachim was fully born that day, for death showed him that time was given only for eternity.

His father had lived over eighty-five years, his spiritual father a little over seventy, but as Joachim stood over the two mounds that marked their graves, he saw how short their long lives were and how empty was the fullest day, if it had not been spent according to God's plan. Life, death, time, eternity, man, God—all took on a newer, fuller, more personal meaning, and Joachim's *metanoia* was complete. His mind was now entirely changed. He had a new set of values for everything from a fleeting moment to a heaped-up year, from a bow to a brother to the managing of the farm, from a single sign of the cross to the marvel and mystery of the Mass. Nothing now was small, for all belonged to the Infinite. Nothing mattered now, for all things were passing; and yet everything counted greatly, for all were parts of his tribute to the Almighty. Now he saw how relative most things are, but the relation that he considered was their relation to the Absolute.

His *metanoia* was complete; for his will had changed. He had a new set of determinations. He no longer resolved to get, he determined to give. He saw that life was for praise, not for pleasure; that every day spent seeking self was a lost day, a day that will never be found in eternity; but every moment given to God would be given back again and live when "skies are fugitives."

His *metanoia* was complete, for his heart had been drained, dredged and deepened, and loneliness gave birth to love. When his two fathers died, both he who had sired him to natural life and he who sired him to the supernatural, Joachim's heart was emptied. But this emptiness was filled and this loneliness changed to love, as into the hollowed-out heart there grew a love for the Father of all fathers.

Falling in Love

Some biographers tell of saints who lost all interest in life and all concern for the world. To them time became a tedium and the world wore a gray, repulsive look. I do not credit such biographers, nor do I believe in such saints. For while there have been sad poets and sad playwrights, sad philosophers and sad historians, sad scientists and sad literators, there never has been and there never shall be a sad saint. Sadness and sanctity do not blend. Sanctity spells goodness and God, and no one who is good and near God can be sad.

As for life, time and the world, all these are treasures to the saint, priceless treasures. Each tiny moment of time becomes tremendously important, for it has been given by God and is to be given back to God. Life and living, though they be replete with suffering and sorrow, with disappointments and defeats, are a romance and a great adventure. Life to the saint is a trysting time with God, or better, "love's brief tournament" in which those who are of God can show their mettle—and win their merits. As for the world, far from wearing a gray, repulsive look, it is flushed with the radiant rose of the dawning and is just as full of bright promise.

It is true that saints long for God and are anxious to see him "face to face," but they are patient souls and are satisfied to see him "in a dark manner" in the world around them, in field, flower and fruit; in sun, moon and sea; in wind, rain and river; but especially in humanity. They long for God with a longing that gives new zest to living, for they know that they can never love and serve God unless they love and serve one another. The saints are absorbed in God. But that is the very reason why they are so mindful of and reverent toward others. They know that God's greatest creation is not the star-studded heavens, not the mysterious and ever-moving sea; not mother earth with her thousand fecund wombs and her dark vaults of precious treasure; not the mountains with their peaks of snow and their veins of gold. Saints know that God's greatest creation is "man," and so saints praise their God by loving "man." No great saint has ever been an idle dreamer or an immobile mummy. The mystic of all mystics, Teresa of Avila, was witty, imaginative and alive. Real lovers of God are intense individuals, perfectly natural, completely human and passionately loving. To them time is never a tedium, it is a treasure—a treasure to be grasped with greedy hands and utilized. The world, from the harmony of the hummingbird's wings to the majestic march of the silent spheres, is a rapture and a revelation. It is the slow but constant unveiling of the beautiful face of their all-beautiful God. No one can sing, "I love life," with more sincerity, spirit and gusto than the saint of God, for he has come to know what "I" means, what "love" is and why "life" is given.

All of which is but a long prelude to the statement that, while Brother Mary Joachim accomplished a perfect *metanoia*, he did not become a mummy or a misanthrope. He kept the same body, the same soul and the same sense of humor. He was John Green Hanning who had set fires, roped steers and blurted a lover's proposal. He was Brother Mary Joachim who had stood guard at the gate with a hayfork, had shaken a menacing razor in an abbot's face and had eaten charcoaled meat. He was the same man who used to "fly off the handle" for the slightest reason, and often it seemed for no reason, but his heart had deepened and he had acquired a newer and fuller capacity for love. The same face was alight in 1890 as in 1870 and in 1885, but now the light was often the radiance of a smile and rarely the blaze of a temper.

From 1890 on, the word "father" meant much to Joachim. In that year he had lost his natural and his supernatural father and, as so often happens, he began to appreciate them fully when it was too late. It is too late to express appreciation when ears no longer hear, too late to show gratitude for countless generosities when eyes no longer see, too late to repay love with love when hearts have ceased to beat. Like the rest of us, Joachim never knew the depths of his love for his dad, nor the wealth of his devotion for Dom Benedict, until he stood over the mounded earth that covered their cold clay.

But this is not the love I had in mind when I titled this chapter "Falling in Love." I was thinking of a higher love for a higher Person, and yet this natural love for his natural father and this human love for an exacting abbot were the source and the secret of his love for the Father of us all.

It should not seem strange that Joachim's extraordinary love for God should have such a commonplace source. All our ideas of God are obtained by analogy or negation. We are only humans, composites of clay and spirit, with minds that depend for their concepts on matter. We cannot know spirit in itself, for spirit has never yet touched the senses. We cannot know the Infinite directly, for the only thing infinite about us is the infinitesimal. What can we, creatures of time who are guided by clocks and the shadows of the sun, know of the Eternal except by analogies and negations? God is spirit, infinite, omniscient, omnipotent, omnipresent, eternal—but we need less abstract words than these if we are to know our God. We need picture-making words, graphic and image-producing words, words that are almost as tangible as fact. And so Infinite Wisdom taught us to pray by saying, "Our Father."

In his own dad he had seen what the forgiveness of a father can be. From him Joachim had learned what the patience of a father can be. A tobacco barn burned, a distillery went up in flames, debts emptied bankbooks, death took half of his heart, life took all of his children and yet his dad had been patient. Reviewing his father's days, Joachim learned what a father's interest, a father's sacrifice, a father's love can be. From Dom Benedict he learned how a spiritual father loves.

The step then from the fathers on earth to the Father in heaven was natural and easy. God became more real, more personal, more fatherly, much nearer. God gradually became God in Joachim's mind and heart—not someone to fear and dread, but a Father to obey and love.

Then the "Our Father" became a prayer, and prayer became a talk with our Father. In the days of Joachim's childhood, prayer had been reverent, holy, awe-filled and pleasant. But with the years, he had grown learned, clever, conceited and unwise. God then became remote, and prayer, awkward. God lived in his consciousness or unconsciousness as he does so often for most of us—entombed. Suffering or the fear of death or some such crisis was needed to make him (as they often are needed to make us) turn to God; and then prayer was mostly prayer of petition. Now Joachim had recaptured the wonder of his boyhood days; he grew young again, young in heart and mind and faith. Now he turned to God easily, gracefully, naturally. Prayer became more than mere petitioning, it became adoring, praising, reverencing and thanksgiving.

He said the "Our Father" with his heart. This prayer of all prayers became meaningful and precious to Joachim and he became a man of prayer. He was suddenly made conscious that God is near, real, personal—a loving Father.

When I say that God became real to Joachim, I do not mean the God of the philosophers, nor even the God of the theologians. There is an ontology about God and it teaches us that he is Being. There is a theology about God and it teaches that he is infinite, omnipotent, omniscient, omnipresent, first cause and final end. But there is a psychology about God, and this images him as the living, breathing, loving, hating, threatening, rewarding, punishing, suffering, lonely, weeping, deserted, disappointed, smiling, honored and beloved God of Abraham, Isaac, and Jacob; the pulsing, heart-thrilling and heart-throbbing God of the Gospels; the merciful long-suffering, just, patient and pardoning Father of Jesus Christ. Not an idea nor an ideal; not a nameless force nor an impersonal prime mover; not a great something, but a Person, a living Person, a loving Person, an intimate—our Father.

This was the revelation that death made to Joachim. It did not come all at once, nor was it entirely due to heaped-up earth that was hiding clay. Many artists had contributed to the perfection of the picture. His mother had started it when she sketched on the baby mind the outline of God, our Father. Silence and song on Texan plains painted their portion, as the thunderous break of the silent dawn and the thrilling symphony of the hushed midnight sky told him that God was over all. Family life gave the rich and warm coloring of love to it. A father's forgiveness etched clearly the smile on the forgiving face of the Father of all prodigals. Gethsemani's abbey and abbot completed the picture as Joachim learned the primary and deepest truth of religion, the fact that the relation between God and each individual is a drama of love. Death uncovered the masterpiece and Joachim read its title with comprehension of its every shade. It read: "God—your Father."

This made our brother a real religious, that is, a man bound to God. Joachim prayed often now; in fact, he always prayed. Formalism was gone. Now he quietly turned and talked to God in an easy, filial way. He knew that God was all around him, that God was in his heart, that it was God who had set the sun shining and who sent the gentle rain, who had given brilliance to cardinal bird and liquid magic to thrush's throat. Joachim saw God all around him. The laughter of the running water and the whisper of wind-ruffled leaves, the flash of bluebird's wing and the call of the evening whippoorwill, all made him think of God. Thus it was that our brother really began to know God, and to know him is to love him!

But do not allow me to be too hurried. In April we may pick beautiful blossoms, but for mellow fruit we have to wait. It is always late August, early September, and sometimes even October, before the delicate white blossom that scented the breeze of April becomes a luscious apple. So, too, with Joachim's love. It was beautiful in 1890—as beautiful as any spring blossom and as delicately scented—but it was not yet the grand, full-blooded, redhearted, passionate love of a man. God works slowly, but he works exceptionally well.

However, Joachim had changed tremendously. His heart was deepened, his mind sharpened, and his consciousness more sensitive and alive to God. All these interior changes had their effect on his exterior. The volcano was not completely extinct, but so deeply slumbering that superiors saw fit to send Joachim to the little college on the hill as prefect.

This, most likely, is the proper place to tell you that Gethsemani College no longer exists, and, strictly speaking, should never have existed; for Trappists are contemplatives and not college professors. Some college professors try to become contemplatives and sometimes succeed, but the process should never be reversed. It does no good to the contemplative and very little good to the college. But when the first Trappists came to Kentucky, almost one hundred years ago, they found the education of the neighboring farmer's sons sadly neglected. So zeal for souls and the charity of Christ for Christ's little ones urged these Trappists to depart from the rigid interpretation of their rule and to start a small school for poor boys. With the years, however, this small school grew and many who were not poor came to it. In fact, when Joachim was appointed prefect, it was a fully equipped college, recognized and chartered by the state of Kentucky. Judged by today's standards Gethsemani College would appear unique. Instead of a college, it would very truly be called a university, for it taught every grade from the first grade grammar to college postgraduate. In 1912, it went up in flames; so the abbot at that time, Dom Edmond Obrecht, could now without embarrassment do what he had longed to do ever since his arrival: he could suppress the college. Loyal alumni and the many friends of the abbey sent in generous donations for the rebuilding of the school, but the abbot returned them with thanks and the statement that Trappists were not teachers. Many excellent Catholic institutions had arisen in the near neighborhood since 1851, and thus the only justification for the existence of Gethsemani College had been taken away.

In 1891, however, the college was in full swing and Joachim and his like were needed to prefect the college boys. I say "boys" because there were very few college men in the enrollment and these few hardly needed a prefect. But the boys—the American schoolboys—they needed prefects, and plenty of them. To such a group Joachim was sent for the express purpose of keeping them controlled and quiet. The majority of the lads were at the noisy and restless stage, and real ingenuity was needed to discipline them without in any way crushing them. Despite his mighty advances in self-control, Joachim now needed very much more of Job's endowment to keep perfect possession of himself. Joachim was still Joachim, and quickly perceiving youth immediately noted two things. One was that Joachim had a temper, and the other was that he had a big heart. The result was that they purposely aroused the temper so that they could profit by the heart. Many a lad was marked "Excellent" in deportment and discipline, just because he had been undisciplined and of very poor deportment.

The great success of Joachim as prefect was gained by winning the boys with his songs of Kentucky and the Rio Grande. With his songs of war and love, he won their love and admiration. Obedience and respect flowed as natural consequences.

Joachim had a heart that was ever ready to fall in love, and during these four years it took many a fall. He loved the lads and the lads loved him, but there was someone else tugging at our brother's heartstrings. Prefecting on the hill had taken Joachim out of the external routine of Trappist living, but only out of the external routine. He kept the internal routine by his fidelity to the two practices that Dom Benedict had given him long years ago. Besides his two offices, those of the Blessed Mother and of the Church, Joachim never allowed a day to pass without making his Stations and saying his Rosary. So what had happened to the word "father" and his falling in love with God, now happened to the word "mother," and Brother

Mary Joachim fell in love with Mary Immaculate.

He could not help it. The grand passion of our brother's life had been his mother. He had loved her from the dawn of reason, and with the years that love had grown.

When in 1882 he had lost his mother, he learned for the first time in his thirty-three years of life how lonely a man can be. In 1891, he found another Mother, someone to venerate, someone to care for, someone to love. In 1891, he found Mary.

There is nothing surprising in this, for one cannot live long in a Trappist monastery without finding and falling in love with Mary. To her the abbey is dedicated, to her are directed the first words that a monk sings in the morning and the last words that he sings at night, to her he chants an office seven different times a day, and to her he flies, as a child to his mother, every time he is in doubt or difficulty.

Mary-love is Catholic. Jesus and Mary, Mother and Son, the crib and the cross are inseparable. If we Catholics did not have Mary as our Mother, Christ would be untrue to his word and we would be orphans; but we have Mary. Without Mary our religion would be psychologically incomplete. The child in us must have a mother, the man in us must have a lady and the knight in us must have a queen. In Mary the child, man and knight find their

FALLING IN LOVE 181

mother, maid and queen, their lover and their beloved. That is why the *Ave Maria* became so precious to Joachim—it was a plea to his Mother. That is why he sang the *Salve*—with so much heart—it was a soldierly salute to his Queen. And that is why his Rosary became so intimate—it was a lover's tribute to his Lady.

It was in these years, too, that the Way of the Cross ceased to be just a set of stations, and became a drama—a vivid, soul-shaking drama—in which his God, who was his Brother, and his Lady, who was his Mother, took the leading roles.

No wonder he fell in love! To have the stations come to life for you: to hear the shrieks of the blood-mad Jews; the words of the weak-kneed Pilate; the splash of the hypocritical waters, as he washed his hands and said, "I am innocent of the blood of this just man"; to have the purple-clad, thorn-crowned, bleeding mess of a Man be someone you knew, someone you loved, to be your own Brother—would you not fall in love?

To see the hard-faced, foul-mouthed soldiery smash this staggering Man, kick him and curse him as they thrust him under a cross that was gigantic; to see him start and sway, stumble and fall; to see the purple-bruised face buried in mud; to see him struggle up, start on, then stop, brush away the blood from streaming eyes and look at a little Lady clad in blue; to hear the two hearts break, and to know that it was all for you—would you not fall in love?

Joachim remembered his own mother and the pain he had caused her when he ran away, and this memory made it easy for him to see Mary's tears and hear Mary's sobs. This fourth station was agony to Joachim, for he realized that he had been the cause of it all.

Thus did the drama go on. Day after day from station to station, from the water that washed Pilate's hands to the water and blood that splashed a soldier's spear, to the water that Mary used to wash the body of her Boy for burial, Joachim saw it all, heard it all, felt it all. It was not a mere memory, nor an isolated historical fact; it was a daily drama, and in it Joachim recognized his shameful role. He realized that it was all for him!

As he stood at the fourteenth station, Joachim was a tumult of emotions. Shame, sorrow and sympathy robbed him of strength even as a rage at his own impotence to change a single act in the long drama fevered his brain. As he saw the lifeless body of Jesus wrapped in the winding sheet and a napkin placed on the eloquent white-red marble of his sacred face, Joachim raged. It was the rage of a man violently in love, and if he could have phrased his will-action at these tumultuous moments he would have said, "Jesus, my King. I'll get even with You!"

Passion must have an outlet and our brother had fallen passionately in love with Jesus Christ. Love must act and Joachim, being Joachim, acted in the only way Joachim could act, he raged interiorly and resolved to do something for Jesus Christ, who had done so much for him. It was Joachim at his natural and supernatural best. He determined to "show God!" He determined "to get even with Jesus Christ!"

The Jesuit mystic, St. Ignatius, said, "Love begets love," and he made love for the God-man the soul and substance of the life of his black-robed legion. The Society of Jesus exists because love begot love in the heart of Ignatius, and the Society of Jesus continues to exist because love still begets love. Christ still captivates souls. Ignatius asked himself—and he would have every Christian continually asking himself—"What have I done for Christ? What am I doing for Christ? What am I going to do for Christ?" Joachim, the Trappist mystic, implicitly faced these questions every morning as he made the Way of the Cross, and he answered them not with words, but with a lover's answer—a beating heart.

Leon Bloy, a French mystic, rightly says, "God is the eternal suppliant for man's love." Joachim, the Trappist mystic, saw this suppliant begging for his love when he saw Jesus Christ fall beneath a heavy cross. He heard this suppliant begging for his love in the awful silence that shrouded Golgotha amid the gathered gloom of Good Friday's three o'clock. Joachim answered this plea with a fierce resolve to prove his love with his life.

Bardaiev, a Russian mystic, truly says, "Man is for the first time at home in the eternal divine-human heart of Christ." Joachim, the Trappist mystic, went home when he climbed in through the side's open wound, crawled down deep into the broken heart of Jesus Christ, and then looked out on life and all things in life with the eyes of the God-man.

Max Scheler, the German convert, wisely says that the fundamental Christian experience of love is expressed not by the theologians, nor the philosophers, but only by the mystics. And I like to think of Joachim as the Trappist mystic, for I know that love begot love. Had he the powers of expression of St. Francis Xavier, I am sure that he would have said, "O Jesus, I love You, for You first loved me."

The Stations of the Cross told of love's furious love, and Joachim, the fiery Southerner, responded. As he stood before the twelfth station, he said something very like what Rev. C. P. Hill, the Passionist mystic, has said in his poem "Turn for Turn."

FALLING IN LOVE

Jesus, my King, I have crucified Thee.
Now, *it is Thy turn! Crucify me!*
Make Thou the cross; be it only like Thine.
Mix Thou the gall; let Thy love be the wine.
Shrink not to strip me of all, save Thy grace;
Stretch me out well, 'til I fit in Thy place.
Here are my hands—felon's hands—
 and my feet.
Drive home the nails, my King, the pain will be sweet.
Raise me! And take me not down 'til I die.
Only let Mary, my mercy, stand by.
And last—let the spear—
 while I live—do its part,
Right through the heart, My King!
 Right through the heart!

Undoubtedly Joachim fell in love, for he was entirely absorbed in God and God's Mother. His mind, memory and will, his whole heart and soul were completely taken up with God, who was his Father, with the God-man, who was his Brother, and with Mary, who was his Mother. And Joachim showed his love in the only way a real man ever shows his love; he showed it by deeds. Love has a language all its own and it is not a language of the lips. If put into words Joachim's love could have taken only one form, and it would have been this:

"I'll show God! I'm going to 'get even' with Jesus Christ." But he did not put it into words; he expressed it the only way love speaks; he told it by his life.

By 1894 Joachim was back in the monastery, and he plunged into the Trappist life as he had never plunged before. Work ceased to be work for him and became a tribute of love. Hard manual labor became a sacrament and a sacrifice for this lay brother of ours who was seeking for some way to say to God with words taken from maturity's wordless but deed-full lexicon, "I love You." Joachim said it, and said it like an adult. He worked with energy to show God that he was sorry for the past, in love with him in the present, and with full hope to love him forever. He worked entirely absorbed in his work and this was absorption in God.

Work is a lay brother's sanctification and his contemplation. He begins it with a dedication to God, continues it with all his energy, just for God, and ends it at the voice of God, the voice of obedience. Lay brothers do not work; they pray and praise God through their manual labor. Or should I say that lay brothers do not pray ordinary prayers—they say those worshipful, adoring prayers of deeds, of duty done, of energetic manual labor? Should I say that a lay brother's fullest and most knightly tribute to his Lady and his Queen is given as he tells his Rosary of love on the salty beads of a true lover's and a true laborer's perspiration.

By 1894, the brothers in the community ceased to be just fellow religious and became, for Joachim, brothers in Christ and brothers of Christ. And so, though some were still sources of irritation, they never knew it. At work there were still some who were slow and awkward and there is nothing more exasperating to the active and the agile; yet the active and agile Joachim was controlled. No more eruptions, no more outbreaks, no more angry signs of impatience. These awkward, slow, and exasperating individuals had become opportunities to say to God, "I'll show You that I get even."

Heart Pearls

There are many who, when reading how a cowboy became a contemplative, will exclaim, "A miracle of grace!" To a certain extent they are right. It was a miracle of grace, and now, in the light of the after years, we can even name the grace that worked the miracle; it was "the grace to be vindictive." But those who exclaim, "A miracle of grace!" are not completely right; and if they mean to insist that it was entirely due to grace that Joachim became the saintly Joachim, they are completely wrong. If one must grow exclamatory and yet wants to hold fast to truth, then one must give vent to a twofold exclamation and say, "A miracle of grace! And a miracle of maturity!"

Vindictiveness does not become virtue overnight. Vindictiveness does not become virtue by grace alone. Vindictiveness becomes virtue by grace and man's cooperation with that grace! It is man's will that makes grace efficient or leaves it merely sufficient. With free will puny man can twist grace, that supernatural gift of God, to a glory, or render this power of Omnipotence, impotent. In their anxiety to give glory to God and to be truly humble, pious souls like to quote, "Without me, you can do nothing," forgetting the while, that it can be said with truth, "Without man, God's grace can do nothing." For every supernatural, meritorious act, the person and God must work together. Without grace, one can do nothing; without the person, grace can do nothing.

Grace was working in Joachim's soul. But never forget that Joachim was working with that grace. Heroic virtue makes a saint a saint; but if this is due to grace and grace alone, why should anyone admire or honor a saint? He has done nothing heroic. God has done it all! And, if sanctity and sainthood are due to God's grace alone, why should anyone strive for sanctity or endeavor to imitate the saints? But do not be so misleading! Remember that a sufficiency of grace is denied no man, but that it is up to man to make it efficient and effective. Man must work! And work as Joachim did!

There were times from 1890 to 1894, when it shook Joachim to the very last atom of his being to keep from breaking out in impatient anger. There were days, and many of them, when the urge to "get even" with certain people tugged and tore at his heart; and countless were the times when southern blood was boiling and southern fires ready to erupt. But they did not. Do not say, however, that grace and grace alone was the fire extinguisher. Be exact. Say that Joachim heroically slaved with the sufficient amount of grace that God gave him, and by his strainings made that grace efficient and thus became a virtuous religious. Salvation and sanctity are not matters of passivity; man must act! God redeemed man, but he does not save man. Man must work, and work hard with the grace that God gives him.

Grace and free will are mysteries; but we do know something about them. After all, it is wrong to deny the doctrine of merit and to say that by praising man for his part in a supernatural work we are detracting from God and the merits of Jesus Christ. Well-informed and thinking Catholics never say that it is the work of God alone, when a man mounts up to the heights of heroic sanctity.

How big a part man's will plays in the production of a meritorious act, I do not know. It may be very small, despite the tremendous effort we experience; but that small part is very important. It is like the tiniest knob on the face of a radio. I can have the radio world's most perfect receiving set, with powerful tubes, sensitive selectors and infallible static eliminators, yet though the air be surcharged with music, not a single note will come from my exquisite loudspeaker, unless I flick that tiniest knob on the radio's face—the tiny knob that turns on the electricity! Joachim's will may have been that tiniest knob, but he flicked it on, and the magic and melody of supernatural works were produced.

Yes, our brother worked hard to attain his mastery. The years down by the Rio Grande taught him what a checkrein was and what it was for. So now, as he labored to make of Joachim a replica of Jesus, he pulled with a vicious hand the checkrein of his will on his mettlesome temper. But do not think that he was only negative. He broke down much, but at the same time he built up. He was not always looking in on self; he was always looking out for others.

This did surprise many. To see Joachim ever on the alert to lend a helping hand was not new; but to see him smilingly, generously, gladly, with a ready and cheerful will, accede to any and every request that was made of him: this was new. Generosity was part of his make-up, but this kindliness, this sweet patience with all and especially with those who were actually imposing on his good nature, was not part of his make-up. It was something that he had acquired, something new, and something that all admired.

A Trappist never gets eight hours of sleep, and the six or seven allowed he takes at a very odd time. Nevertheless, sleep is very necessary for a Trappist, since he works hard and fasts much. Yet when sickness came, and lay brothers or choir religious had to be watched during the hours of the community's sleep, Joachim was the man who volunteered to watch. Joachim was accepted, not because he was strong and could sacrifice his sleep, but because he was calm, gentle and patient, because he had become the pleasant, even-tempered, tolerant and genial Joachim, because he would never grow angry! The community wondered at this Brother Joachim. Here was a completely changed man. Here was a model for the entire community. Here was real virtue and true virility.

I have told you how a Trappist lay brother spends his day. You now know that it is made up of a little reading, more praying and mostly work. It calls for a *man!*

In the days before the Depression, we never heard of the "army of the unemployed." Then work was plentiful and no city was without signs, "Help Wanted." Sometimes the placard read "Boy Wanted," but most frequently it read "Help Wanted" and underneath was added, *"Only men need apply."* Likewise "only men need apply" to become Trappist lay brothers— only real men with hearts of gold and wills of steel. They do not have to be brawny. They do not have to be brainy. But they must be men who can so love God and their fellow men as to forget themselves entirely. They have to be supermen who have wills that are absolutely inflexible, wills that can be screwed to the sticking point of committing a sort of suicide as they bury themselves alive, so that they can live to God alone. Yes, indeed, "only men need apply" for this divine work of building up the Mystical Body of Christ, as they turn their backs on an enticing, flesh-satisfying, ego-gratifying world. Only men, gigantic men, will stay and give to God the glory he wants from creatures he has made to his own likeness and image. Only passionately loving men will stay and die, die to all that man holds dear, in order that other men "might be converted and live." Only men, the boldest and bravest of men, the strongest and staunchest of men, the most fearless and faithful of men, only heroes who want to become saints, need apply for the Trappist lay brotherhood.

Well might a Trappist abbot use the words of Francis P. LeBuffe, S.J., for a prayer as he thinks of the type of men he wants for his lay brotherhood. Well might he say:

> Send me men girt for the battle,
> Men who are grit to the core!
> Send me the best of your breeding;
> Send me your noble ones.
> Them will I clasp to my bosom;
> Them will I call "my sons."
> For I will not be won by weaklings,

Subtle and suave and mild;
But by men!—with the hearts of Vikings
And the simple faith of a child.

Such a man was Joachim. It had broken upon him at last that the Trappist life is not something, but Someone; that it is not a living, but a loving; that it is nothing but being like Jesus Christ.

With this startling revelation, Joachim's heart broke, and from it mists arose, went up into his eyes, blurred his vision, then formed, and fell as heart pearls—Joachim wept! They were not ordinary tears. They did not come from the eyes alone. They welled up from the depths of the soul, for Joachim wept in love. Bewildered by the goodness of God, overwhelmed by the wonder of his Trappist life, astounded by the thrilling realization that he meant much to God, breathless at the revelation that Omnipotence was in love with him, his whole being vibrated. He had to act. He had to do something for Jesus Christ. He had to repay love with love, play turn for turn, and "get even" with God—so his heart broke, broke wide open with love, and Joachim wept—heart pearls.

Were it only once, it would hardly be remarkable. For almost every mortal has his moment, when his soul is so surcharged with emotion that he must weep. Gray-haired mothers and fathers weep at the ordination of their sons, and certainly such an exaltation is no reason for tears. Old age and middle age weep at the first Communion of children, and most assuredly the meeting of innocence with the Innocent is no cause for tears. But such occasions are rare, and such tears tell their own sweet tale. But our Joachim wept more than once. He wept often, and always in the same silent, smiling way.

At Gethsemani, custom has established that in every sermon the priest must make an address to Mary, our Mother. It is not good rhetoric but it is reverence, and some manage to do it quite artfully. But whether it was awkwardly or artfully done, every time Joachim heard our Mother addressed, his eyes glistened, tears formed and fell, and a strong man was offering to the Lady of his life—heart pearls.

During the holy season of Lent, the abbot always chooses some select work on the passion of Jesus for reading in the refectory. Some monks read only with their eyes and their tongues, but there are some who read with their heart. There are some who have voices that are colorless, flat and icy; others have voices that are flame. But to Joachim it mattered not—ice or flame, flat or vibrant—as soon as he heard his Brother's name, he wept.

On the first Sunday of every month a special conference is given, and those who watched Joachim during this period saw his eyes fill, beads form, and beautiful pearls fall—heart pearls for Mary and Jesus, as often as their hallowed names were mentioned by the speaker.

Every night as the shadows creep from the west, the entire Trappist community gathers in the chapter room to hear some spiritual reading; for the day is done, the body is weary and the soul is ready for rest. Almost nightly something would be read about Jesus or Mary and again, as often as they were mentioned, Joachim paid his beautiful tribute of love and joy in glistening tears.

Abram Ryan, the poet-priest, has well said:

Life, only life, can understand a life;
Depth, only depth, can understand the deep.
The dew-drop glistening on the lily's face
Can never learn the story of the sea.

I think those lines give us an inkling of the answer to our question. Why did Joachim weep? It was because he loved. Because he madly loved Jesus and Mary! To paraphrase the poet's words: Love, only love, can understand a love. We, shallow souls with superficial minds and skin-deep hearts, have never grasped the truth that Omnipotence loves us. We have never gone below the surface of God's life and Mary's love. We have never plumbed the depths of Jesus' heart and Mary's soul as did Joachim. So we cannot smile while heart pearls form and fall.

Some name it "the gift of tears," and there is aptness in the name. But these pearls came from Joachim's heart as well as from the hand of God. Joachim had dived deep depths to secure them. He had plunged naked into the dark sea of Trappist existence, and he came up to the surface with heart pounding in his ears, chest splitting for want of air. He came up, blinded and half drowned, but he came up with pearls, priceless, precious pearls, pearls of love for Jesus and Mary that are found in the deep depths of the Trappist's life, when one lives the Way of the Cross, prays his Lady's Rosary, and strives to "get even" with God.

Call it a gift, if you will, but admit that it was a gift well earned. Joachim paid a high price for such a gift. It cost him continual watchfulness, perpetual self-denial, a constant curb on his temper and a driving determination to make his life mold into Someone. We all would weep heart pearls if we would pay the price, the great price of slaying self in order to fall deeply in love with her who is Immaculate and him who is Omnipotent.

But do not think that Joachim was a gloom. Do not think that he was always weeping. His sense of humor had sharpened with the years and the sparkle in his eyes was star radiance. Toward the turn of the century, he was made cellarer of the monastery, which in modern English means that he was supervisor of the farm and buyer for the abbey. This brought him in contact with salesmen, farmers, workingmen and purchasing agents. Of these no one ever left his presence with a feeling of gloom. Most often they left with a chuckle, for men who are close to God are filled with sunshine and laughter, even though they occasionally weep.

One charming little anecdote is told of Joachim's baby sister, Sarah Corina Lee, visiting him. With her she brought her winsome little daughters, Cecile and Mary, for she knew that Joachim dearly loved children and especially these children. After entertaining the children for some time, Joachim turned to Cora and gave her his whole attention, allowing the two tots to amuse themselves around the room. Little Cecile was quite a lady and had on her best party manners, but not so Mary. She was more like her uncle John Green Hanning, and very soon got tired of the confinement of the single room and the droning of these two old people, so she started to rebel.

Neither Joachim nor his sister noticed this, for little Cecile was very old-fashionedly lecturing Mary on the requirements of company. But Mary was not going to take a lecture from her, nor was she going to stay in this one room. She was not going to stay quiet, company or no company, she was going to be herself! Before a real John Green Hanning eruption took place, little Cecile decided to act. She reached up to the holy water font, and soaking her little hand, started to douse her baby sister. Mary did not like it, and she let everyone know it by an outcry that brought the two adults to wide-awake attention.

"What's this?" smiled Joachim.

"Cecile! What are you doing?" scolded the mother.

Then came the earnest, innocent reply to the accompaniment of more holy water, "I'm knocking the devil out of her"—and Joachim roared with laughter. He told that story to the abbot, told it many times, and every time laughed heartily.

It is interesting to note that the little exorcist later became a dignified mother, and from what I heard she had another Joachim in a son she called "Irish." I suppose there were many occasions on which she had to "knock the devil out of him," but I wonder if she did it with holy water.

While speaking of his sisters and their visits, I must tell you of something that Joachim laughed off, but which has me breathless. It recalls very vividly the scene you will find described in every life of St. Bernard—namely

HEART PEARLS 201

that of the saintly Abbot of Clairvaux dictating a letter to his secretary, while all around them is rain, but not a single drop touches the letter. Who can say why God worked such a wonder in Bernard's case? May it not have been so that the story might be told years after, as proof positive that Bernard stood high in God's favor?

I, too, have a story to tell. One very hot summer's day, Clara and Cora, Joachim's sisters, came to Gethsemani. Cora had in her arms little Lester, her baby boy who had just recovered from a severe attack of pneumonia. In the early afternoon the sisters decided to call on friends who lived some twenty or thirty minutes' walk from the monastery. Joachim saw the abbot and obtained permission to accompany his sisters on their visit.

The trip was uneventful. The visit was paid and the little party had started back for the monastery with Cora carrying the baby, when the summer skies suddenly blackened and hurled down a torrent of rain. The mother and aunt looked at one another and then at the baby boy. Fear clutched their hearts, for they felt that if Lester got wet it would mean death. Joachim sensed the situation and with his usual bluff assurance said, "Come, don't worry. Give me the baby, and you two run! You're going to get soaked."

The frightened mother hesitated, but not

for long. For Joachim took the baby from her arms, pointed to the monastery, and said, "Run!" Then he added, "Lester and I will come later. He won't get wet."

The two women ran and, as Joachim had said, they got soaked. For ten interminable minutes faces white with fear pressed against the windowpane watching that empty road. At last they caught sight of a brown-robed brother quietly walking down the road with a white-robed baby in his arms—walking very quietly through the downpour. The poor mother was almost in tears. Joachim was exasperatingly slow and deliberate. Why wouldn't he hurry! At last he was at the step. The door was torn open by the nervous aunt, and the anxious mother snatched a gurgling baby from the arms of a laughing Joachim.

"Oh my poor baby!" gasped Cora, but then she stopped. She felt the clothes of the child all over; then felt them all over again; and then she broke down in tears as she shouted, "Jack! Jack! He's dry!"

And "Jack," who was Joachim, kept on laughing as he said, "Pshaw! You women make me sick. Haven't you got any faith? Of course he's dry. Didn't I tell you he wouldn't get wet?"

It was then that the two women noticed

that their brother Jack was every bit as dry as the baby boy, and they realized that a miracle had taken place. Walking over to Cora's side, Joachim said, "Give me that baby! A fine mother you are! I save the child from a downpour and now you drench him with your tears!" And so he laughed off a miracle.

Joachim "Gets Even" with God

Despite the calm, composed and cheerfully quiet exterior of Brother Joachim, his interior was seething. He was no longer excitable, it is true, but he was still vivid, energetic, passionate. His soul was never more aflame, nor his will more ablaze with fierce determination than now, living his ruby-red resolve to "get even" with God and "to show" Jesus Christ that his infinite love was not wasted, that Calvary and the cross were not in vain. He did it by his Trappist life.

Silence can be a torture, cloister a crucifixion, manual labor an agony, fasting and watching a racking torment, and the Trappist community life a harrowing anguish, if one looks at this as only something. It is not normal, not natural, not human. A human being is not only a rational animal, but also, and very especially, a social animal, the only creature of God on this earth who can speak and laugh—an intellectual animal, the only creature of God on this earth who can think and express his thought. And God himself has said, "It is not good for man to be alone." Yet Joachim was alone. He was silent. Why?

Joachim was normal. He had a heart of flesh, a body of bone, muscle and pulsing blood; he had every instinct common to man. He was human. Self-preservation, self-reproduction, self-expression were three passionate tendencies in the soul of this Southerner, as they are in the soul of every live American. Yet he denied them all. Why?

The roar of the world had often pierced the silence of his soul and, with its passion for practicality, had twisted and tortured the heart of this Southerner as it showed him the futility and the folly of the Trappist life. In its own way it told him that his sublime sacrifice was nothing but a holocaust to outmoded antiquity, a suicide for the sake of an impracticable survival from the Middle Ages. The world frequently asked him, "Why?" It showed him the emptiness of it all, as it asked him what he would have and what he could show for all his silence and solitude. What can a Trappist show to the world? What can a Trappist show to the world that weighs worth in the only scale it knows—that of material accomplishment?

Joachim was an American and he had to face the very American questions, "Why?" and "To what end?" He had not been in the monastery six months before he was asking himself what good he had done for himself, for his fellow man, and for the generations yet to come. What could he do by his Trappist living? These questions were as persistent as Banquo's ghost; they would not be downed.

Joachim was Catholic, and even the Gospel, God's inspired word, gave him pause. He read Christ's parables and was forcibly struck by the parable of the talents. He realized that, if ever a talent could be buried, there was no deeper grave for it than Gethsemani's abbey. As he read the Gospels, he saw that Christ was always calling to an active life. To Peter, James and John, he had said, "Come and I will make you fishers of men." To his disciples he said, "Pray the Lord of the harvest that he send laborers into his harvest. The harvest indeed is great, but the laborers are few." Joachim reflected on the parable of the kingdom of heaven being like a vineyard, and he saw that workers were sent into the vineyard. No matter where he turned, he found Christ counseling action. To the apostles it was, "Go, teach all nations." To the rich young man it was, "Come, follow me," to a life of intense, external activity.

The world with its practiced wisdom and its logical reasoning, the Gospel with its divine revelation, Joachim's own instincts—all made him wonder and ask, "Why?" Where in the

Gospel could he find any injunction to bury himself alive, to live in silent solitude, far from the haunts of men? Christ had said, "So let your light shine before men that they may see your good works and glorify your Father who is in heaven." Where could he find any support for his aloofness and solitude? Certainly not in the story of the Good Samaritan, nor in the one of the Good Shepherd. Joachim had reason to pause many a time and say to himself, "If this Trappist life is saintly, it most assuredly is not the sanctity of the Christ who said, 'Suffer the little children to come unto me,' and who commanded, 'Go into the highways and the byways, and as many as you shall find, invite to the wedding.'"

Why, then, did Joachim stay? What could he answer to this imperative and persistent "Why?" He did answer and he answered fully. He was not a deep philosopher, nor a schooled theologian; he was only an average American, keen, practical and logical. But more, he was Catholic and loving. His full and final answer was given in a name. To that persistent "Why?" that shook his soul down to its bare and unadorned foundations of faith, he answered with a blazing, triumphant "Jesus Christ!" That was his answer to the world and to the devil. It was his full and final justification for living the intense life of a Trappist lay brother. Joachim had come to the magnificent realization that the Trappist life was not something, but Someone, and that Someone was Jesus Christ.

He knew that he had the Christ life—not all of it, but enough to satisfy mortal man. He knew that he could never have the brilliance of Palm Sunday, but he wanted and got Good Friday. He knew that he could never have the pomp and the display of Christ's public life, but he wanted and got part of the passion. He knew that he did not have the whole of Christ's life, but he was happy to have the thirty years of the hidden life and the three hours of the agony.

At the wise world demanding practical results and pointing to the folly and futility of the contemplative life, Joachim could justly fume and point to Jesus Christ. Was there ever such folly as when a God wrapped himself in the poor clay of man's composite, lived unheard of and unknown for three decades, then taught, pleaded, prayed and worked wonders for a stiff-necked people during three years, and as a reward, hung three hours spiked to a cross? Folly? Futility? What material accomplishments could he point to after his life on earth? What tangible results could he show for his thirty-three years of labor and life?

Joachim answered every taunt with "Jesus Christ." The doctrine of the Mystical Body was not so popular in his day as it is in our own, yet Joachim knew that Christ had said, "I am the vine, you are the branches." Joachim knew the world and the ways of the world. Hence, he knew that many branches were broken and some completely dead. He knew that there were souls steeped in sin, so he wanted to be a branch with foliage and fruit; he wanted to be a sinless soul. He knew the besetting sin of society. For six and thirty years he had lived with men and he knew their uncleanness. That is why the words of Christ to his frustrated apostles about a devil they could not expel meant so much to our Trappist lay brother. "Such a spirit is only driven out by prayer and fasting." Remembering these words, our brother felt that he was following the plans of infinite wisdom as he fought in his silent solitude, and he hoped that, by his fighting, he might sire souls as pure as winter's snow, as radiant as the heaven's sun, and as fair as spring-blown lilies. He prayed that from such souls a perfume might arise to heaven, offsetting the stench that goes up from this world that God had made and peopled with individuals with free will.

Joachim could have given many reasons for his staying. There is a threefold division in the Church, and he knew that his futile and foolish life was heaping up merits for the Pilgrim Church, giving continual and efficacious help to the Suffering Church, and paying well-earned tribute to the Church in glory. He might grant that, as far as this world was concerned, there was a seeming uselessness to his Trappist life; but he could demand that everyone admit that as far as those who had gone before him and were in the state of helplessness and soul-searing suffering were concerned, his Trappist life was unspeakably useful. He knew that silence, solitude and celibacy would never populate our vast country, but he also knew that they would greatly depopulate purgatory. And this he considered the greater good.

In time our brother came to recognize this persistent "Why?" for what it really was—a temptation. When it grew very insistent, he rejoiced, for he knew then that he was very like Christ. Satan had tempted Jesus; why should Joachim be immune? And Joachim could have retorted as did the Christ. He could have balanced text with text, paralleled example with example, faced argument with argument. He could have said, "If there must be active Marthas, there must be contemplative Marys. Lights will not shine before men unless there are hidden dynamos. There will be no 'fishers of men' unless there are silent netmakers and unknown builders of boats. There will never be successful preachers of the word, unless there are perpetual pray-ers to the Word. If teachers are needed to tell men about God, there is as great, if not a greater, need for pleaders to tell

God about men. If laborers are to be sent into the vineyard, then there must be branches united to the vine, branches that are filled with the life-giving sap of the vine, branches that are heavy with fruit. If there is to be a resurrection, then there must be a crucifixion. If Christ is to triumph, there must be Trappists."

But Joachim gave one and only one answer. He gave the name of all names—"Jesus Christ." That name was life to Joachim. He knew that, if there was to be Christianity in the world, then there must be other Christs. He aimed to be like Jesus, a voluntary victim for the sins of the world, by leading his Trappist life to the best of his ability. It was his one way of "getting even" with God. Jesus had died because of sin, so, because of sin, Joachim would live what the world called "death." Jesus had satisfied an insulted God and taken away the eternal punishment due to sin; Joachim hoped to satisfy a forgotten God and take away much of the temporal punishment due to sins. Christ was the first and the great Redeemer; Joachim wanted to be another and small redeemer.

Brother Mary Joachim loved humanity as only very few ever love it. He was the greatest of philanthropists, because he was a supreme "Theophilist," a God-lover. Christ said, "Love one another," so Joachim fulfilled that command with love's most terrible proof—death.

JOACHIM "GETS EVEN" WITH GOD

"Greater love than this no man has, that he lay down his life for his friend," said Jesus, so Joachim laid down his life, first for his changeless Friend, then for all his other friends born of the blood of Jesus Christ.

If ever a man was Christ-conscious and Christ-centered, Joachim was the man. He never determined to be kind, gentle and patient. He never resolved to be controlled, genial and humble. He never deliberately cultivated any virtue, but always worked to be just like Christ in everything. He was kind just to be like Jesus; he was patient just to be like Christ, genial only to be like the genial Jesus; humble and meek only because the Christ was meek and humble of heart. Joachim was absorbed in and by Christ, and that is consummate sanctity.

As he made the Way of the Cross, our brother wept often. He loved to linger before the fifth and sixth stations, for he felt that they summed up his life. Simon the Cyrenean had helped Jesus to carry his cross the day that mankind put God to death. Joachim's ambition was to be a "cheerful Cyrenean"; the cross of Christ would not be forced upon him as it was on Simon. No! Indeed, he voluntarily embraced it. He put a very willing shoulder under it, for he knew that mankind was still cruelly crucifying God. Days when he felt exceptionally small, he would stand before the sixth station and thank Veronica for what she had done. Then he would offer his life—not much of a life, just that of an old ex-cowboy, of a vindictive, fiery Southerner, just that of an aging Trappist lay brother—but he begged God to accept it as he had the veil of Veronica, and with it wipe away the spittle of contemporary man from the beautiful but horribly beaten face of our contemporary Christ.

At the turn of the century, when the world was living out its "gay nineties," Joachim was living "Turn for Turn":

> Jesus, my King, I have crucified Thee.
> Now is Thy turn—*Crucify me!*

And he lived his turn with a glory on his countenance and a radiance in his eyes. Silence, obscurity, poverty, penance, manual labor, sweat, chills, humiliations, obedience, denial of self, cloister, abstinence, vigils, fasts at times grated on his soul. Yet he kept the radiance in his eyes and the glory on his countenance, for at such times he felt that he was very specially "getting even" with God.

If God could bear the pain of Bethlehem, then Joachim could take Gethsemani's poverty. If God could become the village carpenter, Joachim could be an ordinary farmhand. If God could love the obscurity of Nazareth, Joachim could love cloister walls. If God could sit by a well, weary from work, then Joachim could sweat under a southern sun. If God could agonize in Gethsemani's garden and die on Golgotha's mount, then Joachim must spike his own soul to the hard cross of silence and solitude, penance and prayer, and "get even" with God by being a perfect Trappist.

In 1907, something new came to Joachim, and he reveled in a new way of "getting even" with God. In the fall of this year our brother began to fail. For over twenty-two years he had been living the life of a Trappist, and for all of those twenty-two years he had been quite well; but now the constitution that had been fired with so many passions began to break up. Bright's disease attacked our Joachim, and he actually rejoiced, for he had a new weapon with which to carry on his combat of "getting even" with God.

Trappist rules grant every consideration to the sick. They can have a private room, can be dispensed from the vigils and the fasts, can even be served meat. But Joachim sought none of these dispensations. Regular order and regular diet would be his medicines, if he had anything to say about the prescriptions; for you see, our brother was suffering from another affliction than that of the body, his pathology was the common pathology of the saints—he was suffering from the enlargement of the heart. He was in love with Christ and the only medicine he could think of for this affliction was the austerity of the Trappist rule.

When the doctor told Joachim that he had Bright's disease, Joachim laughed. And why not? He knew nothing about Bright's disease, but he knew a lot about his other disease and that made him very bright; he knew all about the sickness of the saints—heartsickness. Could Joachim be other than happy and bright? He was close, very close to the loves of his life, Jesus and Mary. He could kneel beneath a sanctuary lamp and smile into the face of his tabernacled God and say, "I'm getting even." You are locked behind a golden gate; I am locked behind monastery walls. You live buried in a wafer of wheat; I live buried in a Trappist home. You are a silent God; I am a silent monk. The world pays little heed to You; it laughs at me. You live in bread to feed my soul; I live in brown to comfort Your heart, my Captain Christ. You died for me; Jesus, my love, I live for You! Joachim was happy.

Even the worldly world should understand that. For she ever teaches that the only way to be happy is "to know what you want and then, go get it!" She is a practical world and she teaches her children the direct, ruthless, determined method of "Go, get what you want. Count not the costs." She is an efficient and an effective world. Her principles she puts into practice and her pupils are always apt. I have seen an Edward give up England and a Carol forfeit Rumania in order to have the women of their hearts. The world had taught them not to count the costs. "Know what you want," she had said, "then go, get it!" That is the language of the worldly world, and that is why I say she should understand Joachim's happiness and should roundly applaud his Trappist life. He had taken her principles and put them into practice. He had forfeited all right to empire and resigned the realm of the world in order to have the loves of his life, the Queen and the King of his heart.

The great Depression showed how lasting is wealth. Power can be lost overnight, as the Czar of Russia, the Emperor of Germany, the Kings of Italy and Spain so bitterly learned. Prestige and popularity are as long lived as the ever changing moods of a very fickle people. Worldly pleasures are as ephemeral as smoke. But had there been no depression, no revolutions, no changing moods, even then, the human heart would not be at rest, for this world offers nothing that the human heart can permanently possess. Death is ever the grim specter which laughs at graspy, greedy humanity and makes it realize that its efforts are as futile as Tantalus' labors. Wealth goes, for there are no pockets in shrouds. Power and prestige go—where are the Caesars of yesteryear? Popularity goes—man's memory is very short!

But Joachim had what he wanted, and he could have it and hold it forever! He had grasped God. He had the Infinite One for friend and lover. In Gethsemani he had him in a veiled, sacramental way; but he had him. In heaven he knew that he would have him unveiled, face to face, and forever. Hence even the worldly world should understand the happiness of this lay brother, who spent his life in a contest of "getting even" with God.

The fall of 1907 had faded into winter and winter had melted into the spring of 1908 as Brother Joachim, despite his fifty-nine years, despite his Bright's disease, despite his almost twenty-three years of Trappist austerities, went on radiantly living his rollicking romance of "getting even" with God. He felt his years, he felt his disease, he felt his hard life, but above all, he felt his heart and that was pulsing at an ever higher tempo and sending a richer and a redder love through all his veins, urging him to live his seventeen- and eighteen-hour day more earnestly and all for God. He arose, read, prayed, and worked with the others. Not only did he refrain from complaining, but he actually hid behind a sunny smile all the wear and tear of sickness and time.

The holy season of Lent came and our warrior wanted to take it in stride. He wanted to live on one full meal a day, add to his prayers and his penances, and work shoulder-to-shoulder with the youngest. He wanted to spend this Lent as he had spent twenty-two

JOACHIM "GETS EVEN" WITH GOD

other Lents, in the closest union possible with the Man of Sorrows. Joachim wanted to give his all in imitation of him who had given his all. Jesus had come to mean so much to Joachim that a day without some special sacrifice for him was a wasted day, a day entirely lost. Lent then loomed as a glorious season for our love-filled Southerner, and he began it with southern fires flaming and southern temper at its best—determined "to show" Jesus! And he did—for a few weeks. But shortly before Passion Sunday, the superiors saw that their volcano was just about burned out, so, though it hurt them to do it, they called "Halt," and ordered Joachim to the infirmary and to bed.

John Green Hanning would have violently exploded to have his plans thus ruthlessly upset, but Brother Mary Joachim straightened up, drew in a long breath, and after a moment during which a southern jaw was set, he broke into a radiant smile, thanked his commanding superior and went to bed. It hurt the old man, but even this hurt he made into a joy and chuckled to himself as he was given a room and said, "Now I'll really get even."

There are many lonely places in the world; graveyards are lonely, asylums are lonely, hospitals are lonely, but the loneliest of all the wide world's lonely places is a Trappist infirmary. To some that statement may come as a surprise, for they will wonder how men who have spent their entire lives in silence and solitude can become lonely. But that surprise and that wonderment comes only from a lack of comprehension of the Trappist life.

A Trappist lives in absolute silence, it is true; but a Trappist lives in community. There are men like yourself at your elbow. Their eyes speak; their bodies move; they are alive and full of energy. They work with you, eat with you and pray with you. They become part of you. They are your closest of close companions, even though you have never spoken and, most likely, never will speak a word to them. A Trappist is not a hermit, not a solitary; he has the continual, close and congenial companionship of men like himself, who are striving with all their puny might to give something to God. Hence, when he is sent to the infirmary, away from the community, away from the community exercises, away from all contact with his fellow monks, he knows a loneliness that is fearful. Joachim saw what was ahead of him when he was ordered to bed, he saw that he would be lonely as the God of Golgotha was lonely, so he chuckled and said, "Now I'll really get even."

For thirty days Joachim stayed in bed, and for thirty days he peopled the silence of his lonely room with a King and a Queen. He said his Rosary continually as he now walked his own Way of the Cross. He missed the community as much as Christ missed his apostles in Gethsemani and on Golgotha, and so a pleasant little smile was always playing around his lips—he was actually "getting even" with Jesus Christ. Mary was with him, as she had been with Christ. But she was not his *Mater Dolorosa;* she was the cause of his joy. Boy, man, and monk rose up in him as he gave his heart's devotion to his Mother, Maid and Queen; so, despite his consuming determination to "get even" with God, he began to grow very homesick for heaven. Joachim was always a home boy, and twenty-three years of Trappist living had shown him his true home. This knowledge now culminated in a sigh-filled nostalgia.

A Trappist never fears death. Why should he? To him it is not the end, but the very beginning of life, his gateway to God. He knows that the angel of death is Christ, and that death's summons is but the command of the King of kings and the Brother of brothers to "come home." Why should he fear death? He has lived life for God alone, and death gives him God. For the Trappist monk death is not darkness, it is dawn! For years he gropes in the outer darkness of our little whirling planet, straining to grasp God. He sees him only in a dark manner, no matter how bright the light of faith. Then comes death, and what is it but the thunderous break of the eternal dawn?

They say that a hard life makes an easy death. If that proposition is convertible, and I believe it is, then Joachim must have had a very hard life, for he had the easiest of deaths. On April 30, 1908, he fell asleep. The priest who was attending him noticed the peacefulness of the slumber and the pleasantness of his smile. From that sleep, Joachim never awoke. He fell asleep on earth to open his eyes in heaven.

At last he had "gotten even" with God. It took him twenty-three years to do it, but he did it. Perhaps the pleasant little smile that played around his lips that last day was caused by his mind saying, "I'll get even. I always do." And maybe our Lord Jesus Christ, who has an infinite sense of humor, greeted Joachim not with the usual, "Well done, my good and faithful servant," but with, "Welcome, my American Vesuvius. You've gotten even at last. You always did! But now it is my turn."

God "Gets Even"

Brother Mary Joachim died on Thursday, April 30, and was buried on Friday, May 1. You see, Trappists do not mourn their dead. Why should they? If ever the euphemism, "Gone to God," was true about any mortal, it is true about Trappist monks. They live for God alone; could their deaths be anything else but a "going to God"? So why should they wake their dead or mourn over them? Why not rejoice?

Tears fell, it is true. Tears fall at every Trappist death, and at every Trappist burial; but they are tears of loneliness, touched with the salt of envy. You conceive a tremendous love for these men to whom you never speak, but with whom you live in closest communion. Your hearts become entwined as no other human hearts do or can. Your minds, your wills, your souls have been busy about the selfsame Object all your Trappist life. Your days and nights have been spent side by side, doing the identical thing. Your whole lives, from the moment you entered the monastery, have been cast in the one mold, and human hearts, being human hearts, fall in love. It is more than an ordinary love—more than that of comrade for comrade, friend for friend, or even brother for brother. It is more than any human love, for it is touched and tinted with the divine. Somehow or other, these men become part of your very self. Perhaps it is the unity and solidarity of the Mystical Body really felt and actualized. Whatever it is, heartstrings become entwined in a holy love. Death snaps those strings and so there are tears, but no real mourning. Tears fell when Joachim died, for his going made everyone quite lonely.

His worn-out body was placed on the Trappist bier and carried to the church. There, lighted candles were placed at the head and the feet, for this was holy clay. Then in the mellow glow of the candlelight, two white-robed choir monks sat and recited unendingly the psalms of the psalter. From the moment that he died until the solemn Mass for the dead began, two white-robed monks, succeeding one another at half-hour intervals, sat by the body in brown and recited those inspired prayers of King David.

Friday morning the solemn Office for the Dead was sung and then a solemn Mass. After the Mass, the community formed in solemn procession and led Joachim's body to its last

GOD "GETS EVEN"

resting place, that sacred square where iron crosses sentinel the holy sleep of sacrificial love. Song floated on the scented breeze of May and, as monks bent prostrate, their eyes were wet but their voices were steady and strong. Over the grave an iron cross was planted, a silent sentinel for his sacred dust. His fellow soldiers fired a triple volley over his grave, but it rang out from throats and not from muskets, as they put their hearts in the thrice repeated song, *Domine, miserere!* "Lord, have mercy!"

The echoes died in the breeze of May; the last shovel of earth fell on the dank mound, and seemingly all was ended. But not! God is never outdone. Joachim had "gotten even" with him, now it was God's turn. Two months had not passed when a letter came from the outside world. It was a letter from a lay person who had come in contact with Joachim when he was prefect at the school and cellarer of the monastery, a person who had seen holiness and love for God shining in the fun-loving eyes of this Trappist lay brother and who, on hearing of his death, had started to pray *to* and not *for* Brother Mary Joachim. This person wrote that a novena had been made in honor of our brother, and that on the ninth day of the novena heaven had answered. God was "getting even" with Joachim, but it was only the beginning.

God is still "getting even" with Joachim. People in and outside the monastery have prayed to this American Trappist hero, and have not been disappointed.

For example, there was a nun who, after long years in the service of God, felt spiritless and uninspired. It was April, 1939, a time when the whole world was bursting into new life and breaking into bud. The universe was trembling with spring's ever thrilling, miraculous activity. But all this new energy and festivity of nature only increased the listlessness in the soul of this good nun. By the end of the month she was destitute of all enthusiasm for life and living, when suddenly she thought of Joachim. This was his anniversary: April 30. So she turned to him and asked him to obtain the grace she needed. She did not specify. She hardly knew what to ask for, so she simply said, "the grace I need."

That very night, try as she would, she could not fall asleep. She tried to pray; she tried to plan; she tried to think, and tried to fall asleep again; but every attempt was a failure. Then quite suddenly and out of nowhere, there came into the very center of her soul a picture of a vine with branches. Some were healthy and heavy with fruit; others were half broken and starting to wither; still others were entirely dead. She looked uncomprehendingly for a moment, and then, with all the force of a revelation, the whole purpose of her life, her part in the Mystical Body, was made startlingly clear to her. She arose, and falling on her knees vowed again her all to labor unto the end for the Vine and his branches. Her heart was loud in its throbbing and her eyes were very wet as she turned to Joachim and thanked him for one of the greatest graces she had received since childhood.

There are many who have a touching devotion to our brother, but none shall ever surpass that of his baby sister, Cora. It was she who had witnessed the "miracle of the rain," for Lester was her child; it was she who had learned from her older sister Nannie of Joachim's "gift of tears." These facts coupled with her many visits to Gethsemani and the truly inspiring letters she used to receive from there, convinced her long before 1908 that her big brother, John Green, was near and very dear to God. Hence, when death came, she made a little shrine for his picture, and every evening after praying to him would tell him a fond "good night." When trouble came, she had recourse to her big brother in trustful prayer, and trouble left her. When her little ones were going to school, she had special work for Joachim. She called on him, told him to take care of the youngsters, to accompany them to and fro, to keep them out of dangers and especially to keep them from getting wet. Ohio's Valley has many sudden shifts in weather and very much rain, and yet, before her death, Cora said that not once in all those years did her little ones come home from school wet. Joachim was faithful. All this was God's way of "getting even" with the man who always "got even."

Is it any wonder? Could God refuse a man who had slaved for years with the one fixed purpose of "getting even," of giving back love for love, of bearing suffering for suffering, of crucifying self because God had been crucified? Could God refuse anything to this American who had buried himself alive so that he might live to God alone? Could God refuse anything to a man who, cooperating with his grace, had twisted vindictiveness into a virtue and from a flaming Southerner had become a fiery saint? Hardly!

And God is still "getting even." For example, just as we were going to press for the first printing, a letter arrived with this petition: "Will you please have Brother Joachim pray for me? I know that he is dead and has been dead for years. That is why I ask you. I feel sure that he is in heaven and can greatly help me. He was such a grand saintly brother, God must love him."

I agree with that writer, "God must love him," and I agree with another writer that "saints are given us for admiration." Need I tell you that I admire Joachim? Need I tell you that I consider him a saint?

Speaking of sanctity and admiration—did you know that just about the time that Joachim was "getting even" with God, the whole world was whipped to admiration for another saint by the writings of Robert Louis Stevenson? This was the time that the heart of America stood still, and the head of America bowed in thrilled tribute to Father Damien of Molokai. Stevenson drew an unforgettable picture of a man who abandoned all self-interest so that the outcasts of human society might be served by a man with God's sacraments and God's Sacrifice. Damien was a hero, a saintly hero; and even the most bigoted bowed in acknowledgment to the gigantic unselfishness of this priest of God.

Would I surprise you were I to compare Joachim with him? Well, I do so; and now I give my reasons.

Far out in the blue Pacific, removed from all, stands Molokai, the land of the leper, the land of the living dead. To that tomb Damien went so that he might serve those whom society had outlawed. There Damien died; for he contracted the dread disease from those he so unselfishly served; and Molokai had its first martyr. When the memory of this magnificent man was sullied, Robert Louis Stevenson wrote a work in which he showed the giant courage, bravery, heroism and heart of this priest of God. Through his work the world saw a lover of humanity lay down his life for its outcasts; and all the world paid homage.

For once, the world was right. And I would not take a jot or tittle from the tribute given this heroic priest of God. But I would have you contrast him with Joachim.

Damien lived and died for lepers. Damien lived and worked with lepers. But Damien was thanked and blessed by lepers! Bodies might be rotting, but souls were sound; and souls shone out in lepers' eyes and souls spoke out from lepers' tongues. But what recompense did Joachim have as he lived and died in the land of the living dead for lepers—the spiritual lepers of human society?

There is no Molokai for spiritual lepers; but there was a Joachim! He buried himself alive, voluntarily isolating himself from all. He stripped himself naked of self and selfishness, that spiritual leprosy might be cured and spiritual lepers live again through God's Sacrament and God's great Sacrifice.

Damien gave up much when he went to Molokai; but Joachim gave up more. Damien had the consolation of absolving penitent lepers, converting ignorant lepers, feeding starving lepers, helping dying lepers and solacing suffering lepers. And from these lepers, day in and day out, he may well have heard: "God bless you" and "God love you" and "I thank you." But what of our martyr of silence? Did spiritual lepers ever say to him, "God bless you, Brother Joachim," "God love you, Brother Joachim," or "I thank you, Brother Joachim"? Did eyes ever shine upon him with love, or lips speak their affectionate appreciation? Did hands ever clasp his calloused and work-worn hands?

Molokai is cloistered by the sounding seas, but never as deeply cloistered as Gethsemani. There Joachim slaved for twenty-three years without ever a single soul saying, "Thank you." Spiritual lepers were cleansed. Their souls shone again with the glow of ruddy health. But they never knew that a lowly Trappist lay brother had won them their miracle. Hence, they never thanked him. On faith alone Joachim lived and for twenty-three years slaved for others without a shred of human consolation.

They tell me that of late years much admiration has been stirred up for "Brother" Dutton, the Civil War officer who hoboed his way across the country, stoked his passage from San Francisco to Honolulu, and then, with ecclesiastical and governmental permission, went to help Damien at Molokai. Three years later, when Damien was dying, he made Dutton promise that he would never desert the lepers. Dutton promised, and for forty-one years he lived his promise! When asked how he stood it, he smiled and simply said, *"I love them."* That is heroic love! Yet I say that Joachim out-Duttoned Dutton.

Dutton had a Damien to talk to for over three years; Joachim had only silence. Dutton had human beings to work for, leprous human beings, it is true, but still human beings who had human hearts and human words and human love; Joachim had only spiritual souls.

To have lived and died at Molokai is high heroism. Unquestionably. What then shall we say of the heroism of him who lived and died at Gethsemani?

Yes, "saints are given us for admiration." But this is very wrong if it means that they are *only* for admiration. Leon Bloy is right when he says, "We *become* nothing," if he means that we work with, on and through the individual human natures God has given us, if he means that a blustering Simon could only become a fearless, outspoken Peter and never a mild and quiet-spoken Nathaniel. But Leon Bloy is wrong and very, very wrong, if he means that we are *born* saints and do not *become* such. For Joachim has conclusively proven that a boy who always "got even" with everyone, can become a man who "gets even" only with God. He has most clearly shown that Americans are not doomed to a spiritual mediocrity; that if they will go down to the depths of their hearts they can scale the heights of sanctity. And finally, he has shown to all that a cowboy can become a contemplative, a flaming temper can be a favor from heaven, and vindictiveness can become a virtue.

Long silent in life, brother Joachim now speaks in these pages for all to hear.

Foreclosing—Joachim Speaks for Himself

I began this book with a "Forewarning." It was necessary. I end it with a "Foreclosing." It is just as necessary. You had to be forewarned and protected against yourself. I must foreclose and be protected from others; and Joachim will do the protecting.

For quite some time I have been face to face with the besetting sin of hagiographers—exaggeration. From early youth I have read lives of saints. Some won my admiration and others stirred me to imitation, but not a few produced nausea! Now saints are not sickening. But many authors of saints' lives draw so exaggerated a picture of their subject that they afflict one with mental dyspepsia. They completely dehumanize their saint, making him or her anything but a being of flesh and blood, representing the saint either as so austere as to be positively forbidding, or as so gentle, kind and charitable, as to be absolutely unpalatable.

However, I think that I have diagnosed

their disease. They are sufferers from heart trouble. They fall in love with their subject, and their heart rules head. Love leads them into lyricism and we get a subjective dream that is very distorted instead of a portrait of objective reality.

But a life of a saint should not only open our eyes and open our mouths; it should lift up our hearts. When we ordinary mortals have read the last line, we should not be amazed. We should be determined and say with Augustine, "If they can do it, so can I!" A saint's biography is not to entertain and amuse: it is to stimulate and infuse new life, new fire, new determination to be what we should be—saints. We should close the book saying, "This person was a human like myself, with flesh, blood and bone; passions, pride and blind impulses; faults, failures and many defects. But this person won his way up! I can do the same." For this the saint must be depicted as one of us, human.

But these rhapsodizing authors would lead us to believe that the world is made up of sinners and saints. It is not! It is made up of sinners who recognize God, and those who do not; of sinners who admit their sin and do penance, and those who do not; of prodigals who return home, and of prodigals who still stray. A saint is one who belongs to the first class. Too many of us belong to the second.

There have been those who preserved their baptismal innocence. These we congratulate and envy; we cannot emulate them. But the vast majority of saints were converted sinners, and so we can grasp them by the hand and say, "Lead me on!" They not only open our eyes and mouths in wonder, they lift up our hearts in hope.

Saints with souls that have never been sullied may stir us to awe and holy envy, but they will never set us fighting our way up to God. Actually, they can discourage and dishearten; for looking at them, we feel that at best, we can be only mended vases—vases that show to the discerning eye the cracks and clasps, the varnish and glue, that tell the tale of a wholesale shattering. These sinless saints make us think that we are blighted blooms that can never come to a perfect flowering. It is untrue! He who has fallen deepest can climb the highest, for he starts from lower down! Peter was not given the primacy until after he had denied the Lord. Paul was made the "vessel of election" only after he had been shattered to fragments by his hate of the Christians. When sinners return home, they are not relegated to the rank of servants, but are given a ring for the finger, shoes for the feet and the robe that is called the "first"!

I suppose that you are wondering just why I titled this "Foreclosing," "Joachim Speaks for Himself" and then blithely went ahead to do all the talking myself. There is a reason. I have done much talking for I have much ground to clear. I have shown you a sinner who scaled the heights. I have taken you from the depths to dizziness, from a raging temper that broke hearts to tears that were heart pearls. Some will be tempted to say, "Exaggerated! Joachim and John Green Hanning are poles apart. Such extremes could never be had in the one individual. And even if such a sinner could become such a saint, he could never maintain the humanness claimed for him." That is why I must let Joachim speak for himself.

I have said that Joachim wanted to "get even" with God, and have insisted that his twisting of vindictiveness into virtue was the molding of the sinner into the saint. Read this letter, dated January 31, 1908, addressed to his sister Mary Katherine:

My dear Little Sister,

I am in possession of your letter ...and feel so thankful to God that you are cheerful and contented. Earth becomes a paradise to one who is perfectly conformed to the holy will of God. Cultivate a great love for this virtue in your heart, and you will experience a joy which hitherto you have not known.

Everyone has to suffer in this world, but *Oh, how sweet it is to suffer for One whom we love!* When once you have tasted the sweetness of this divine love, you cannot afterwards be contented without it. It is the only true happiness that we can have.

I told you that our brother had become most generous and full of consideration for others, didn't I? This is what Joachim wrote in the same letter:

> Others may seem to be happy and joyous, but if you could read the secret of their hearts, you would judge quite otherwise. Therefore always be kind to others, no matter how they may treat you. Try to win them to love and serve God; for their trials oppress them, and not knowing how to suffer for the One whom they should love, they are rendered miserable and deserve compassion.

And Joachim gives the reason for this consideration and compassion when he adds:

> Thus your work will become like that of an angel, or rather, like that of Jesus Christ himself.

Have you noticed the date on this letter? It is just three months before his death. I am now going to give you its last paragraphs and its "P.S." He writes:

Through the hours of the day, from the pearly dawn until the starry dark, and through the quiet watches of the night, in heartfelt prayer, I am pleading with sweet Jesus through his Blessed Mother, for my dear brothers and sisters and their families—all of whom are his precious treasures and whom he loves with an eternal love—to the end that we may praise his holy name and share his joys forever in heaven. Continue to frequent Communion; it will be your greatest comfort in life and at the hour of death. Nourish your precious soul with it, for it is infinitely more necessary than is food for the body.

Kiss dear Josie and Sim and all their family, and Ella, little Babe, and John for me. I pray for you and all your good intentions.

With a heart full of love for each and every one of you,

Lovingly,
Brother Joachim

P.S. I become more and more happy every day. It is my opinion that life will soon end for me in this world.

After her husband's death, Mary Katherine was seriously thinking about becoming a nun. In a letter of reply, Joachim gives us his ideas on the religious life.

FORECLOSING—JOACHIM SPEAKS FOR HIMSELF 241

> My dearest Little Sister,
>
> I always bear you in my heart and in a special manner in my prayers, Holy Communions, etc., pleading with our dear Lord to bless you; but never have I dreamed of the extraordinary grace that you mention. It would be the greatest blessing, honor and dignity that you could receive. To become spouse of Christ, queen of heaven and mother of God are dignities beyond expression. And you would become all three: spouse, because betrothed to him by the vows of poverty, chastity and obedience; queen of heaven, because the spouse of the King is Queen; mother of God, because you cause him to be born in the hearts and souls of others by your prayers and good works.
>
> ...If you only knew the great dignity to which our Lord has called you, you would not need counsel!

Do you remember what I said about Joachim's going to Gethsemani? I said he did so because he wanted to be great. Do you notice how he insists on the honor and dignity of a religious vocation in this letter? Twenty odd years had not changed his notions! This is how he continues that letter:

> Experience alone can teach the great peace of soul the religious life gives during life; and it is an assurance of a happy

death. Out of a community of about seventy who were here when I came, there are only three left. I have seen many of them die, and all died sweetly. All were aged men.

Now comes a beautiful picture of life and death in religion. Taking up the sentence "Out of a community of about seventy who were here when I came, there are only three left," he says:

The youngest of the three is about seventy years of age and he is perfectly blind (perhaps you think I am too, for I am writing in the dark), but he is perfectly happy. He has become familiar with the monastery and can go where he pleases; besides, in such a large community there is always someone ready to give him special attention. He is cared for like a tender mother would care for her child; for charity, brotherly love, is one of the virtues we hold most dear. He had splendid sight when I came, but he has become blind of late years. He is a priest and says Mass daily; I often serve him. I am not allowed to speak to him, but I will have you remembered in his prayers and 'mementos.' I speak of him that you might contrast his life here with what it would be in the world, where everyone is seeking pleasure and flying from cares and trouble. As I have said, brotherly and sisterly love is one of the chief virtues of a religious, and to assist one another in bearing his cross is a delight. But how different it is in the world! Besides its many dangers of sin, let one become dependent and life becomes insupportable.

The picture is well drawn and the clash of contrasts sharp. But Joachim had become the saintly Joachim; hence the prime motive of all his actions was love.

My dear Little Sister,

Our dear Lord has called you to his loving heart. Take shelter in its sacred wound, and thus receive your eternal happiness. Life is but a dream, eternity an everlasting reality of happiness or suffering. Let us secure heaven now that it is in our power.

Learn to love God with all your heart! He has created heaven and earth and all things for love of you, and has given his life and the last drop of his precious blood all for you. Now he offers you a place beside him as queen. Accept it! Accept it for his greater glory, and your own dignity and eternal happiness.

I would never finish, if I were to say all that I would like to, but will leave the rest to sweet Jesus. Hoping that he may pierce your heart with his dearest love.

Bro. Joachim

In every letter I find him in awe at the fact of Christ's infinite love and that astounding proof of it—the shedding of his blood even to the last drop. This is how he opened a letter addressed to two of his sisters:

> My sweet Little Sisters,
>
> I received your dear letter, and was happy to know that God was lavishing his choicest blessings on you both. I have answered that letter many times in my heart, but have deferred a written answer in compliance with our holy rule.
>
> You both, and all the souls of those whom you love, grow dearer to my heart day by day. But what is my love, or the love of any creature for you, when compared with the infinite love of our sweet Redeemer, who has shed the last drop of his precious blood all for you?

This wonder and awe at God's infinite love as shown in the passion absorbed Brother Mary Joachim. The only other thought that occurs with like frequency is the contrast between time and eternity. You have already seen that beautiful line, "Life is but a dream, eternity an everlasting reality—of happiness or suffering"; he has another one equally beautiful in a letter which gives his philosophy of sorrow. He writes:

> Sorrow is the substance of man's natural life. But as under every stone there is

> moisture, so under every sorrow there is joy. Sorrow is but the minister of joy. We dig into the bosom of sorrow and find the gold and precious stones of joy. Sorrow is a consideration of time, but joy is the condition of eternity.

This particular letter was written March 3, 1908, just three weeks before he took to his deathbed. I give you his closing lines to show you the thought that was uppermost in his mind, for I want you to see the joy that was in the heart of this hero who goes to meet death with a smile.

> Never be discouraged, my dear little sisters. Against all your trials battle bravely for the joys which await you; for you have a place in the Sacred Heart of Jesus and he has prepared a throne for you in heaven, the beauty and splendor of which infinitely surpass the conception of man.
>
> I am so happy that I cannot express my joys.
>
> Lovingly, your brother,
Bro. Joachim

It is easy to see why Joachim was so happy. He knew that he had "a place in the Sacred Heart" and that there was a "throne for him in heaven." This very same thought he expressed to Mary Katherine in this fashion:

> If we only knew the sublimity and grandeur of the end for which we were created, how joyous and happy we would be! How our hearts would overflow with the sweetest love for our dear Lord, in gratitude to him for having chosen us from among so many other souls for such exquisite bliss that it is beyond the power of words to express or the mind to conceive.

And now I come to a page which Joachim penned *from the infirmary:*

> With regard to my health, I think that it is very good, though my superiors and doctor are of different opinion. The consequence is that I am in the infirmary. God's will be done! I am indifferent regarding the matter. As long as I am candid with them in expressing my belief, they may do with me as they please. One thing is certain. I am happy and grow more so every day.

That the doctor and superiors should consider him a sick man, sick enough to be confined to the infirmary, is a great joke to Joachim. He even shares the humor of the situation with his superiors. But they refuse to see it; so with a twinkle in his eye and a chuckle in his voice, our brother bows to their will and goes to bed.

FORECLOSING—JOACHIM SPEAKS FOR HIMSELF

This particular letter he meant as some sort of a "last will and testament," for in it he bares his soul as never before and shows the twin loves of his life, Jesus and Mary. You remember that when Joachim first came to the religious life, he was almost too proud to beg; well, as the end approaches he is humble enough to beg for pardon and for prayers.

> I have but one fear and that is that I might become another Judas. Do pray that I will continue in the hope of the mercy of God and in the protection of our sweet Immaculate Mother.
>
> I now beg pardon of you and Cora and all your dear little pets for all the pain I have ever given you, and I hope that God will reward you for all your patience with me.
>
> Hoping that God may ever bless you and lead us all to a happy union with him in heaven; praying for you and in union with you for all your good intentions, with a heart teeming with love for each and every one of you, I am
>
> Devotedly your brother,
> Bro. Joachim

This love for family is found in every letter that survives. Sometimes it is an exclamation, "Oh, how confidently I hope and fervently pray that we will all meet in heaven, never more to part, to see, know, love and enjoy God forever!" Sometimes it is an exhortation, "Let us secure heaven while we may." But most frequently it is just an admission. "The greatest part of my work is intercession for those near and dear to me"; and again, "I am pleading with the sweet Jesus through his Blessed Mother for all my brothers and sisters and their families, that we may praise his holy name and share his joys forever and ever in heaven."

But Joachim's love was not limited to those on earth nor circumscribed by family limits. You have already seen something of his love for others. You have read his ideas about sorrow and suffering and the world's great need of sympathy and compassion; he also thought of the other world. To Mary Katherine he says, "It is a great charity to pray for the poor souls and the conversion of sinners, and to have a Mass said for them whenever you can." To Clara and Cora he was more explicit, saying, "Do not fail to have Mass offered now and then for poor souls and for poor sinners." And of himself he often says, "I do not forget any of my relatives or friends in my prayers." "I never forget them (relations) nor anyone near or dear to them in my prayers; I also pray for an ever increasing love for all my dear friends." "It is only through intercessions for man, in union with Jesus, that we can render any true service to our fellow creatures."

You remember that there was a time when

FORECLOSING—JOACHIM SPEAKS FOR HIMSELF 249

John Green Hanning sat and sneered at the most solemn part of the Mass. Listen to him now as he tells what Brother Mary Joachim thought of the adorable Sacrifice. It is the Feast of Corpus Christi. He is talking to his sisters, acknowledging their letter with its request that Masses be offered. He writes:

> My dear Little Sisters,
>
> I received your letter in due time, and your Masses were promptly attended to. By these Masses you have offered to God the greatest glory possible.
>
> Tempestuous oceans and towering mountains, murmuring brooks and silent valleys, dark forests and smiling plains, fields of waving corn and blooming meadows, singing birds and roaring lions, the earth clothed in its floral beauty, the cerulean hue and the bright sunbeams of the firmament, the flying clouds and the majestic, rolling thunder, the vivid lightning and the mysterious quiet reflection of the nightly world of stars, and beyond the stars—there, 'the abode of the blessed with their canticles of praise,' and the angels, those indescribably beautiful and exalted spirits, those morning stars and firstfruits of creation, those princes of heaven, whose brightness outshines and dims all earthly splendor, as the sun eclipses the stars—and finally, the Virgin Mother of God, the glorious Queen of

> angels and saints, from whose pure heart
> issues and shall eternally issue forth the
> ecstatic, joyous chant of the *Magnificat*—
> all these in united praises cannot render
> to God the glory of one single Mass! Yes,
> one single Mass procures God more
> honor and praise than all the worship of
> all the citizens of heaven and earth can
> offer him throughout eternity!

I defy the diffused but captivating Fr. Frederick William Faber to do any better than that. Of course, Joachim was very fond of Faber and was continually begging his sisters to secure and read *All for Jesus* and *Bethlehem*, two of Faber's most famous works. Hence, it may well be that our brother borrowed much of the above from Faber. If so, then I congratulate him on his excellent taste; if not, then Joachim astounds me! However, the rest of the letter is genuinely Joachim.

> On this memorable day, Corpus
> Christi, twenty-two years ago, I came to
> this monastery. I participated in four
> Masses for you and dear Cora today, and I
> offered all my prayers and Holy Communion for you. When the thought of our
> sad parting at home would come to me, I
> could not keep back the tears. How I long
> to meet you all in heaven, where we will
> never part again!
>
> I ardently pray that Charlie and Lester (two nephews) may become priests. If

they only knew the great honor and dignity of the priesthood, both here and for all eternity in heaven, they would fly from the world to its fond embrace. And for sweet little Cecile (niece), I pray that she may choose for her spouse our Lord and Savior, Jesus Christ, that she may be happy in time and robed in nuptial robes of gold, seated on her queenly throne beside the King of kings for all eternity.

Has Joachim spoken enough for himself? Twenty-two years had deepened his love for his family and his longing for God. He could cry as he recalled the past, but a rainbow would shine through the mists of those tears as he looked forward to heaven. For nephews and nieces, for brothers and sisters, for sinners and the souls of the departed he had only one desire: that all get closer to Christ! In this he proved himself truly THE MAN WHO GOT EVEN WITH GOD.

St. Paul Book & Media Centers

ALASKA
 750 West 5th Ave., Anchorage, AK 99501 907-272-8183.

CALIFORNIA
 3908 Sepulveda Blvd., Culver City, CA 90230 310-397-8676.
 1570 Fifth Ave. (at Cedar Street), San Diego, CA 92101 619-232-1442.
 46 Geary Street, San Francisco, CA 94108 415-781-5180.

FLORIDA
 145 S.W. 107th Ave., Miami, FL 33174 305-559-6715; 305-559-6716.

HAWAII
 1143 Bishop Street, Honolulu, HI 96813 808-521-2731.

ILLINOIS
 172 North Michigan Ave., Chicago, IL 60601 312-346-4228; 312-346-3240.

LOUISIANA
 4403 Veterans Memorial Blvd., Metairie, LA 70006 504-887-7631; 504-887-0113.

MASSACHUSETTS
 50 St. Paul's Ave., Jamaica Plain, Boston, MA 02130 617-522-8911.
 Rte. 1, 885 Providence Hwy., Dedham, MA 02026 617-326-5385.

MISSOURI
 9804 Watson Rd., St. Louis, MO 63126 314-965-3512; 314-965-3571.

NEW JERSEY
 561 U.S. Route 1, Wick Plaza, Edison, NJ 08817 908-572-1200.

NEW YORK
 150 East 52nd Street, New York, NY 10022 212-754-1110.
 78 Fort Place, Staten Island, NY 10301 718-447-5071; 718-447-5086.

OHIO
 2105 Ontario Street (at Prospect Ave.), Cleveland, OH 44115 216-621-9427.

PENNSYLVANIA
 214 W. DeKalb Pike, King of Prussia, PA 19406 215-337-1882; 215-337-2077.

SOUTH CAROLINA
 243 King Street, Charleston, SC 29401 803-577-0175.

TEXAS
 114 Main Plaza, San Antonio, TX 78205 512-224-8101.

VIRGINIA
 1025 King Street, Alexandria, VA 22314 703-549-3806.

CANADA
 3022 Dufferin Street, Toronto, Ontario, Canada M6B 3T5 416-781-9131.